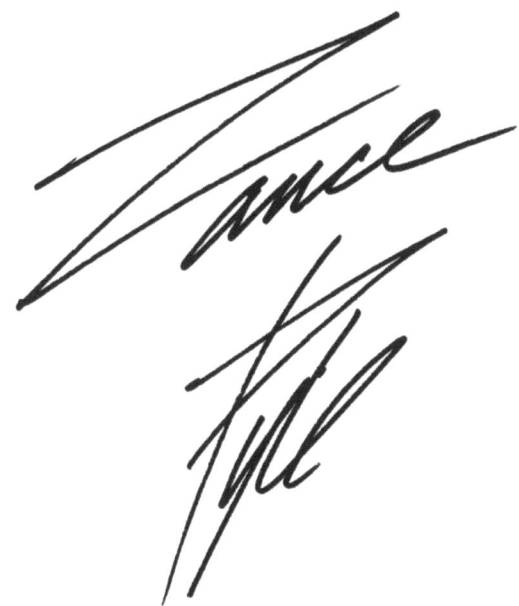

Of art, architecture & poetry

To Rose

Lance Pyle – Of art, architecture & poetry

© 2018

All rights reserved. No part of this book may be reproduced in any manner whatsoever without the written permission of the author except in the case of brief quotations embedded in critical articles and reviews. Printed in the United States of America - Scary Black Goo Publishing – P.O.Box 647, Sacramento, CA 95812

ISBN 9781720518570
Library of Congress number 2018906862

I want to acknowledge:

My parents and family for their belief in me,

The professors at the University of Oregon and the University of Kansas for structure and routine,

And the professors at CCA, California College of the Arts, formally CCAC, who taught me how to reach the inner gardens of my creative potential and to see the small things that can go on-noticed,

So, don't blame me, this is all their fault!

Preface

"The ability to laugh holds the power to heal much"

I've had cancer several times now, and since I'm still here I figure I might as well put together some sort of visual memoir least I be gone tomorrow.

The Accidental Journey

In 2008 My-Old-Life walked over to the side of the road and sat down. It was weary and out of breath. But it looked up and smiled as My-New-Life now began to walk by. Cancer had taken most of my tongue - I had to learn to speak again. I desperately needed to find a place within me where the pain didn't exist anymore; where the cancer had made no purchase. I needed a new point to start from, a place where I could walk and rest and dream if I wanted to, and to hear the music that I knew had always been there. . . . *AND* what I found had always been there. I just needed a desperate reason to go find it. It's a place inside us all. *It's a place where the laughter dwells and the flowers grow.*

OF ART

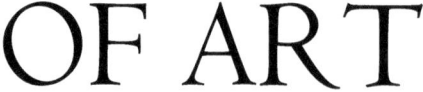

1968 – 2018

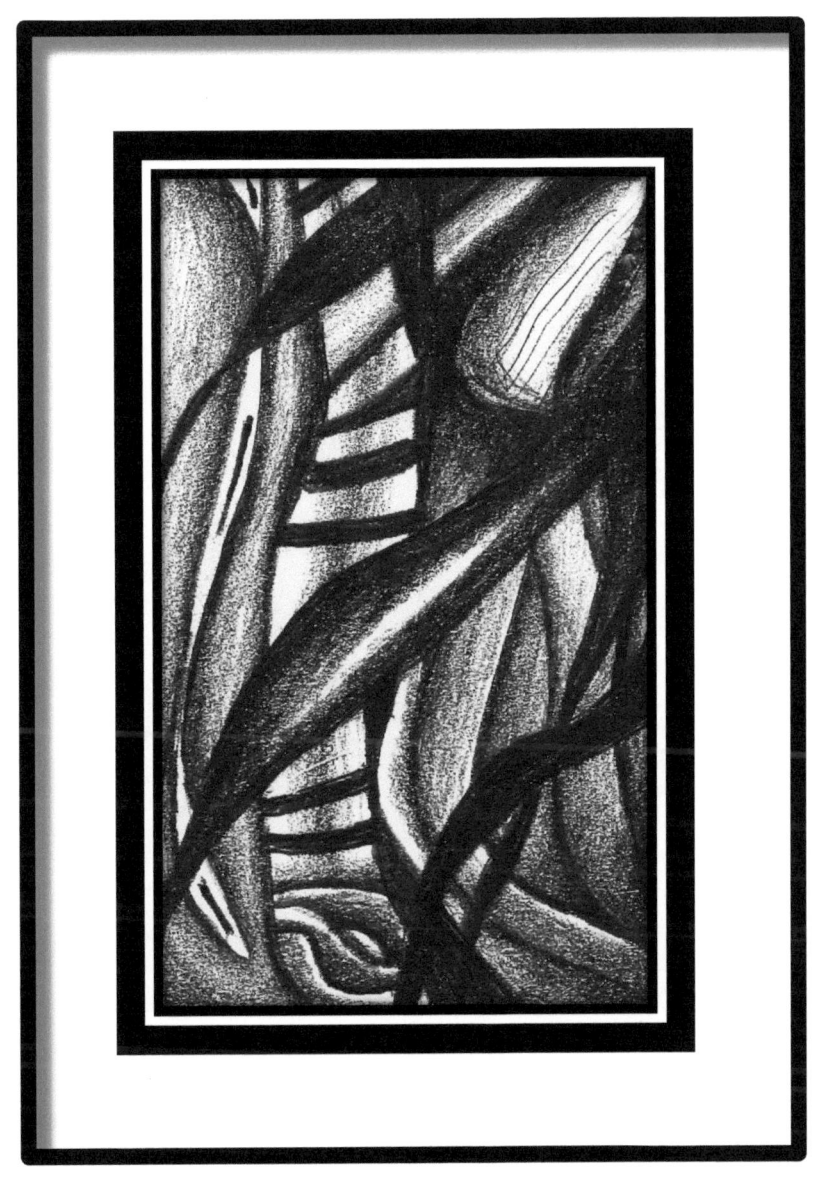

The Snake
3.5 x 5 pencil on paper

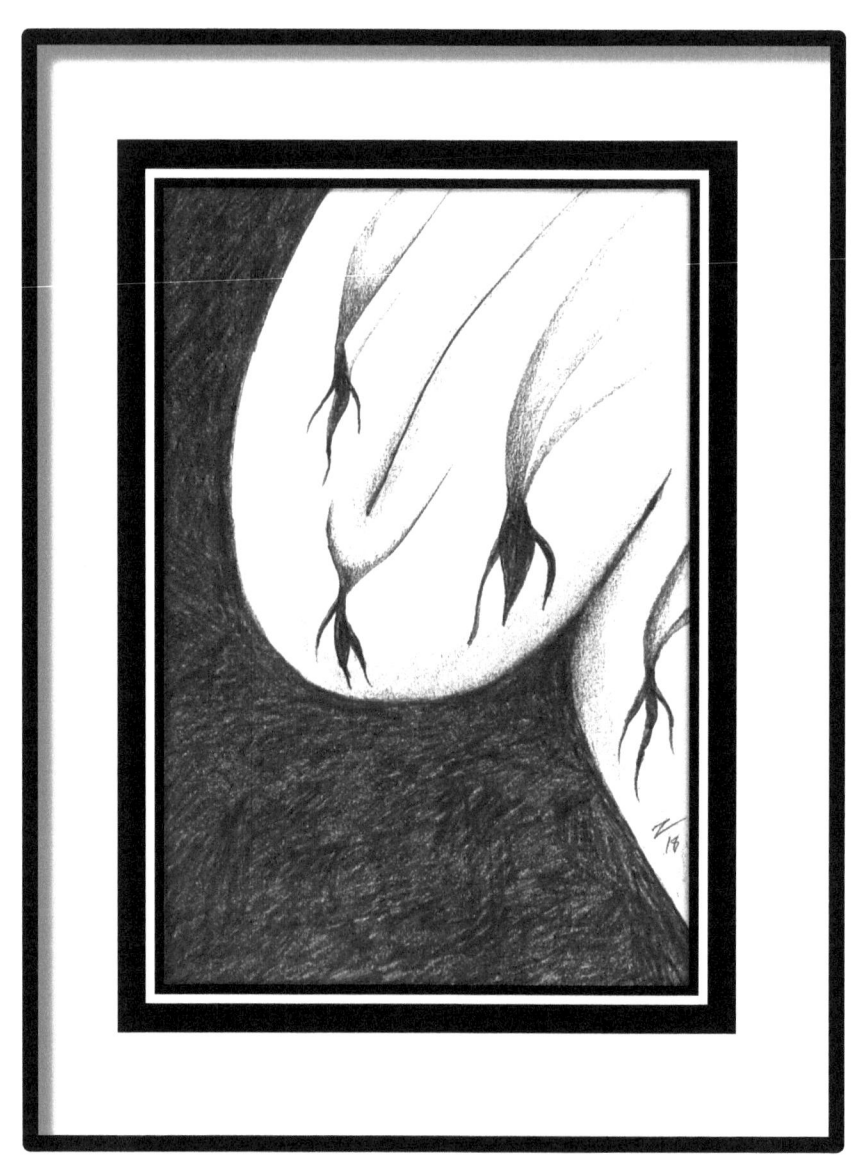

Primal Creep
5 x 7 pencil on paper

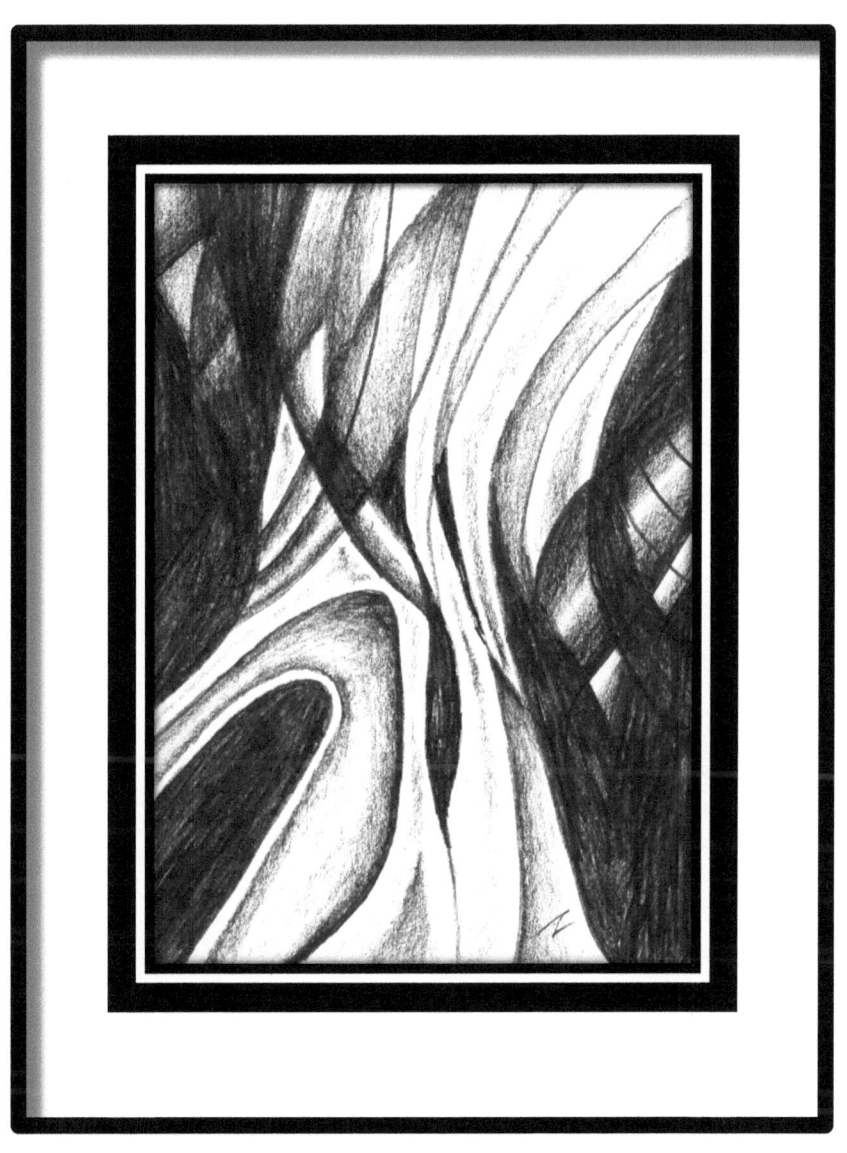

When The Wind Blows . . .
"*the grass moves and what's hidden within is seen.*
5 x 7 pencil on paper

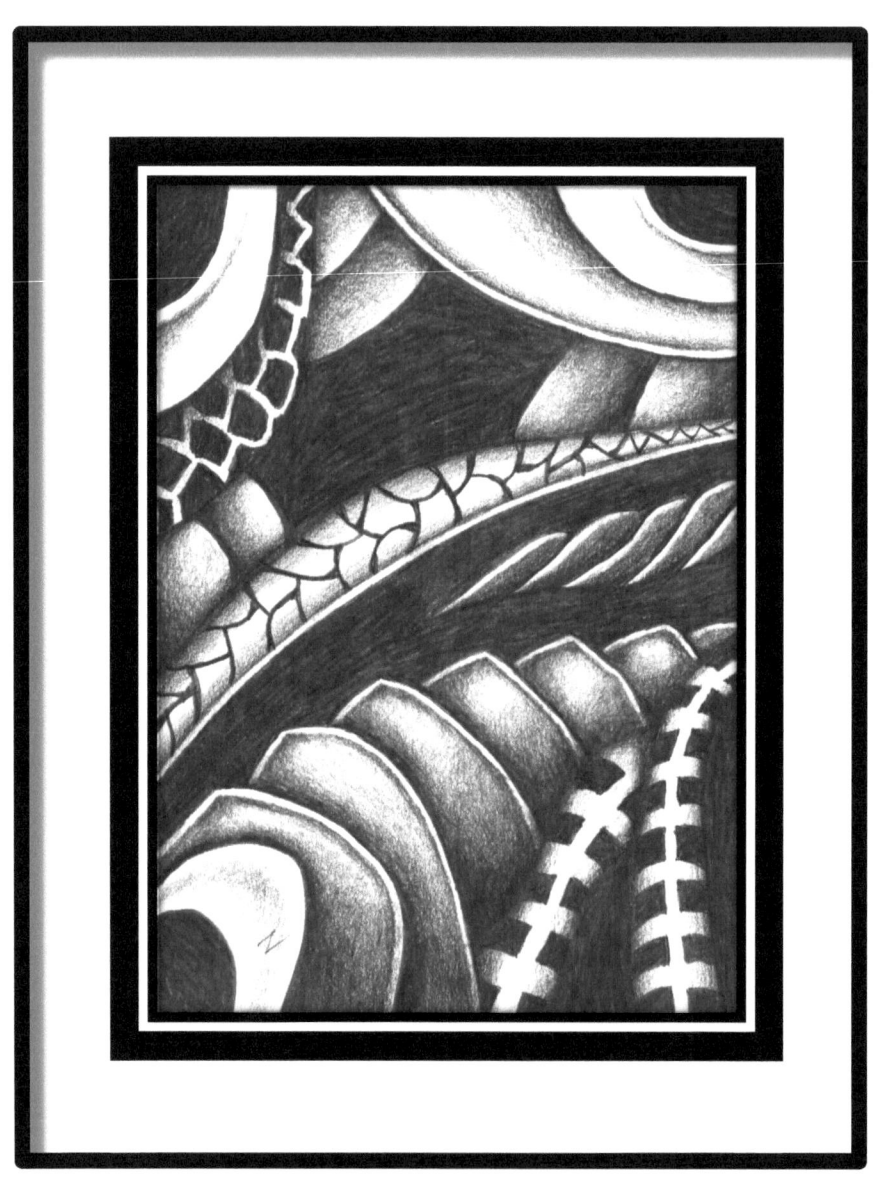

Seven Steps
6 x 9 pencil on paper

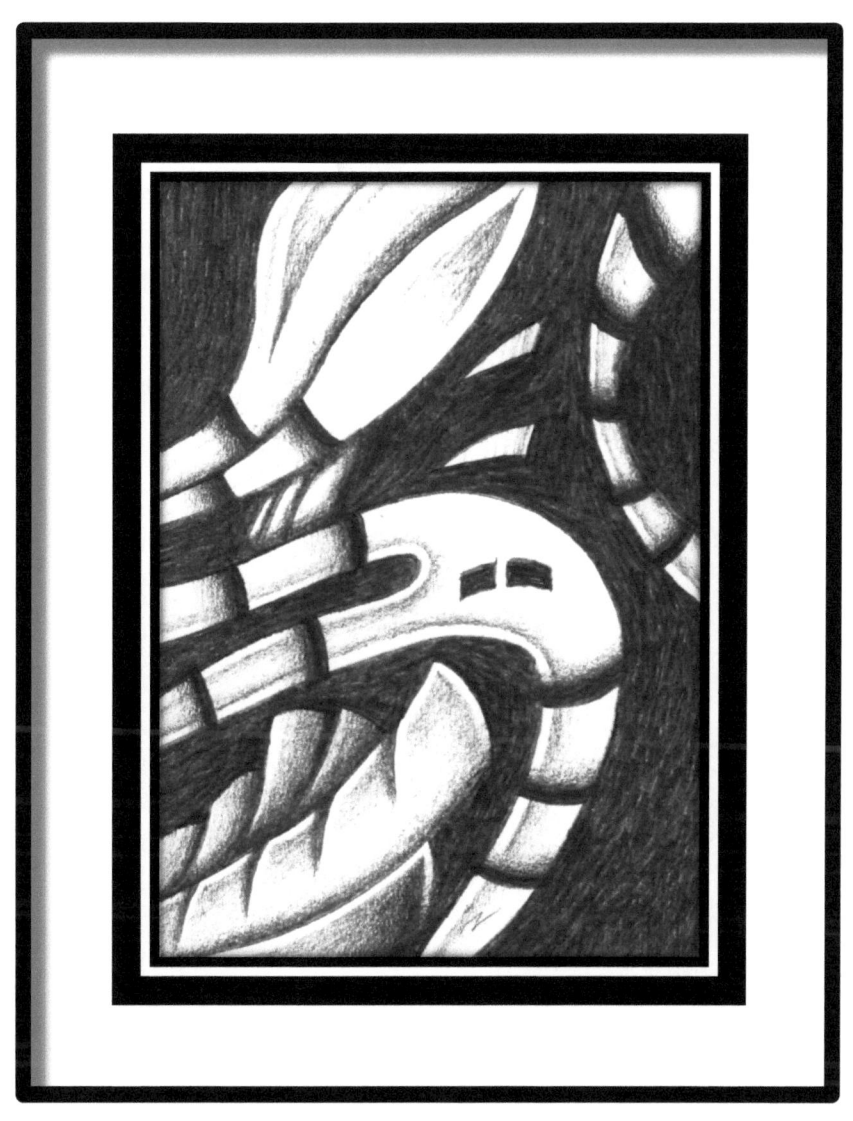

Crocuses And Snakes . . .
"on French Bread"
5 x 7 pencil on paper

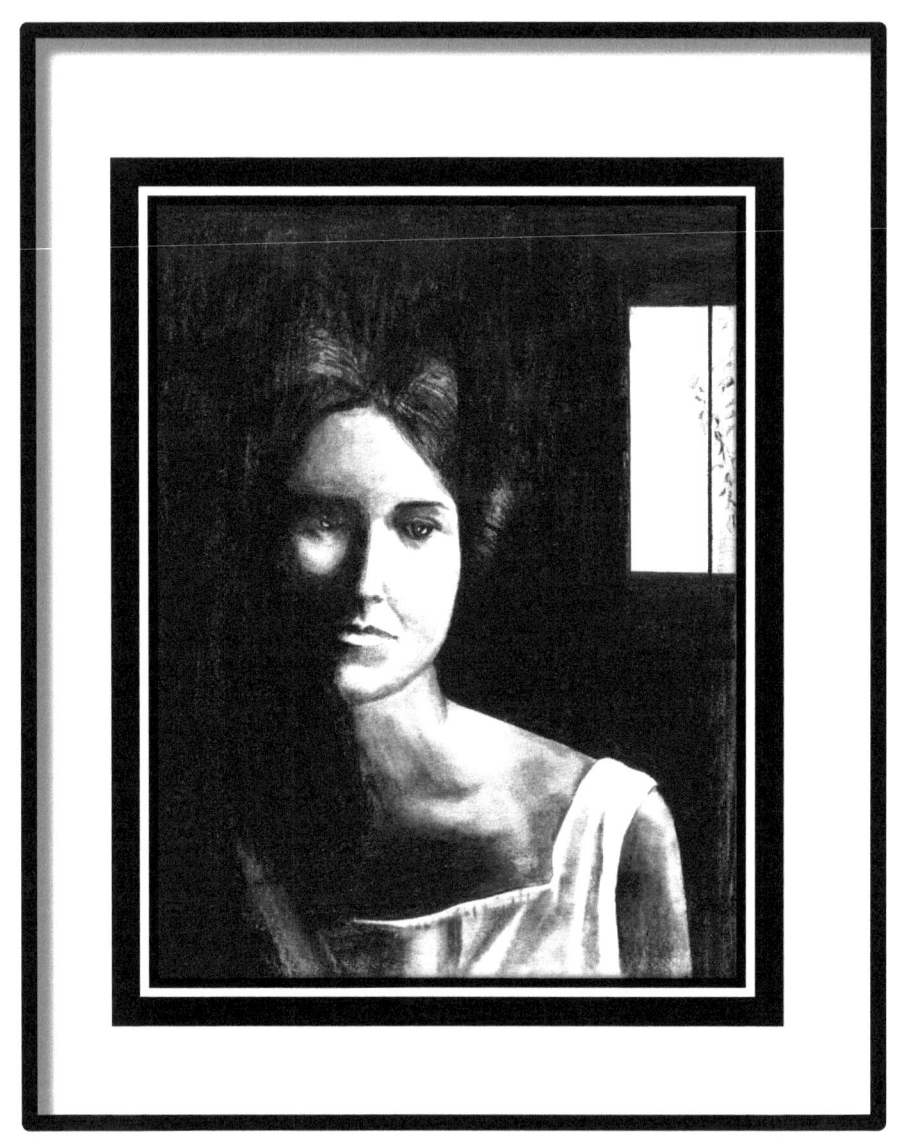

September
6 x 9 pencil on paper

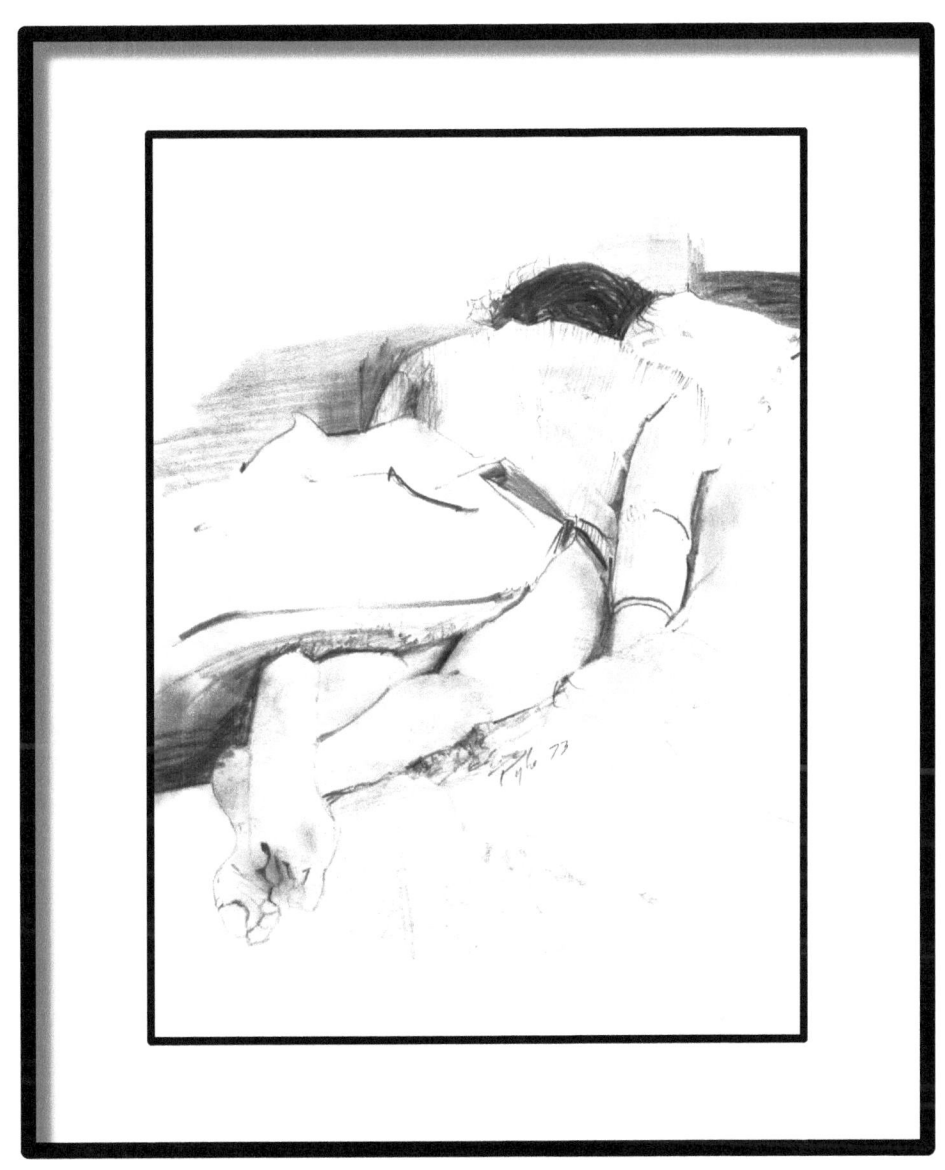

While She Sleeps
8 x 11 pencil on paper

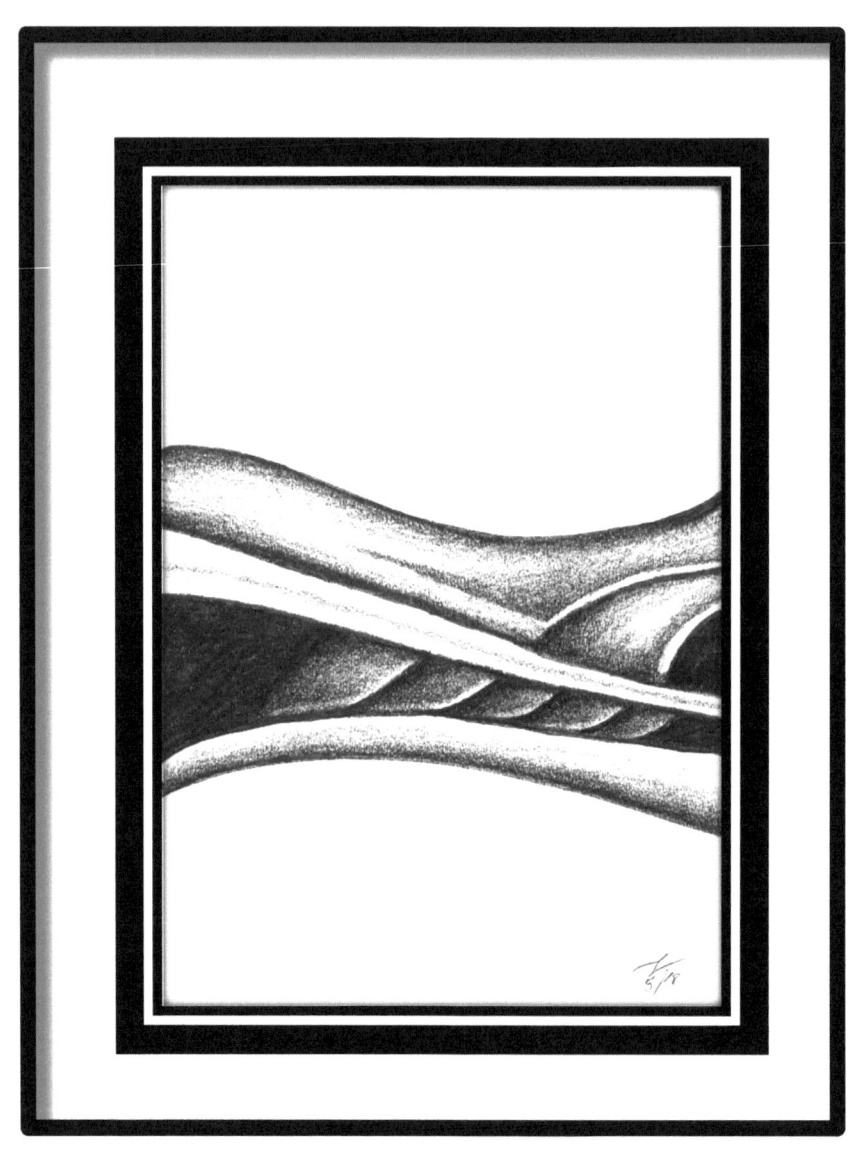

The Space In-Between Here And There
5 x 7 pencil on paper

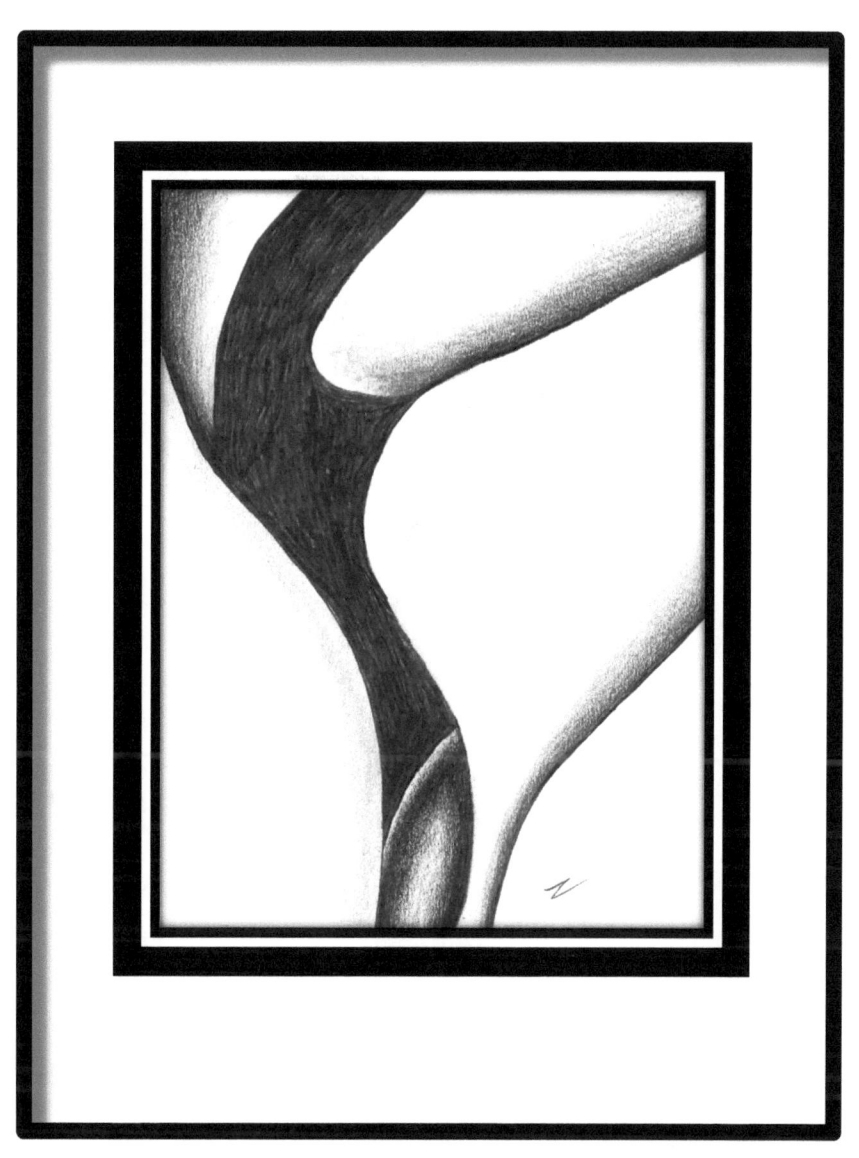

The Rise of Her Inhibitions
5 x 7 pencil on paper

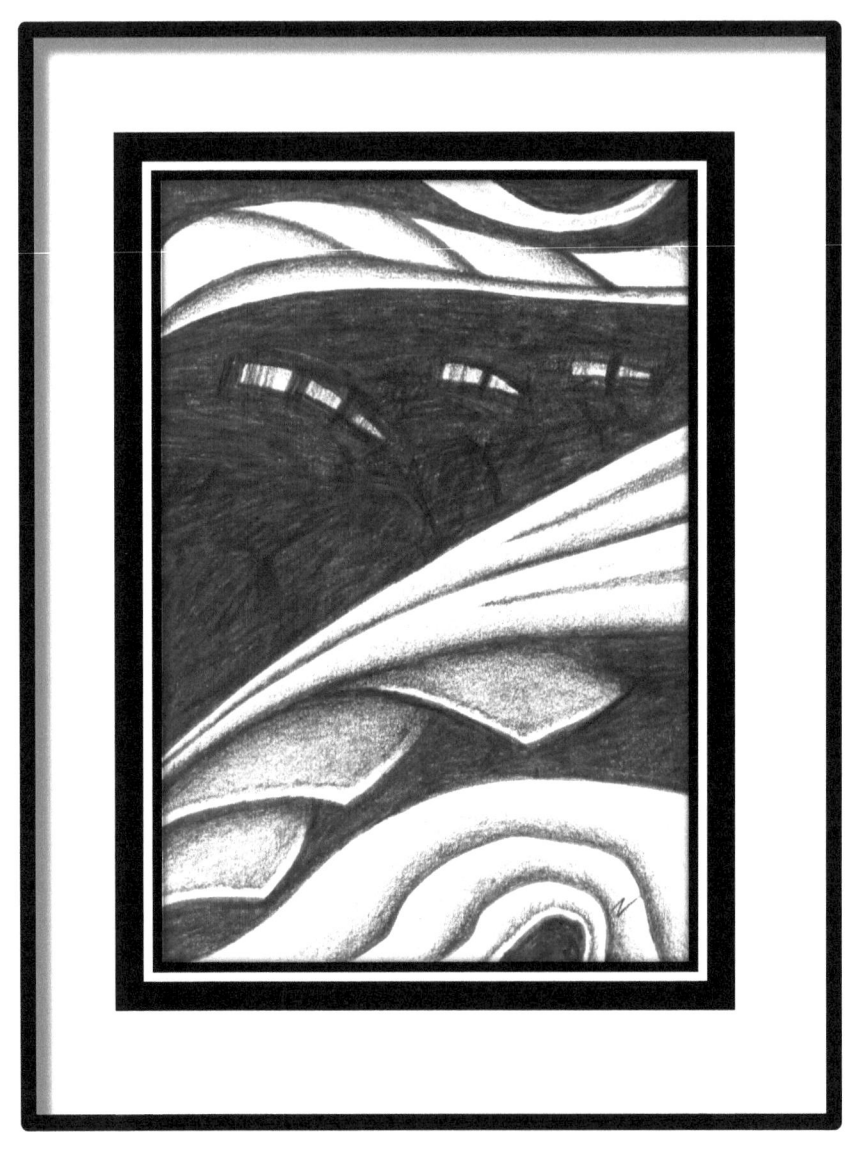

Three Dreams Looking For A Place To Land
5 x 7 pencil on paper

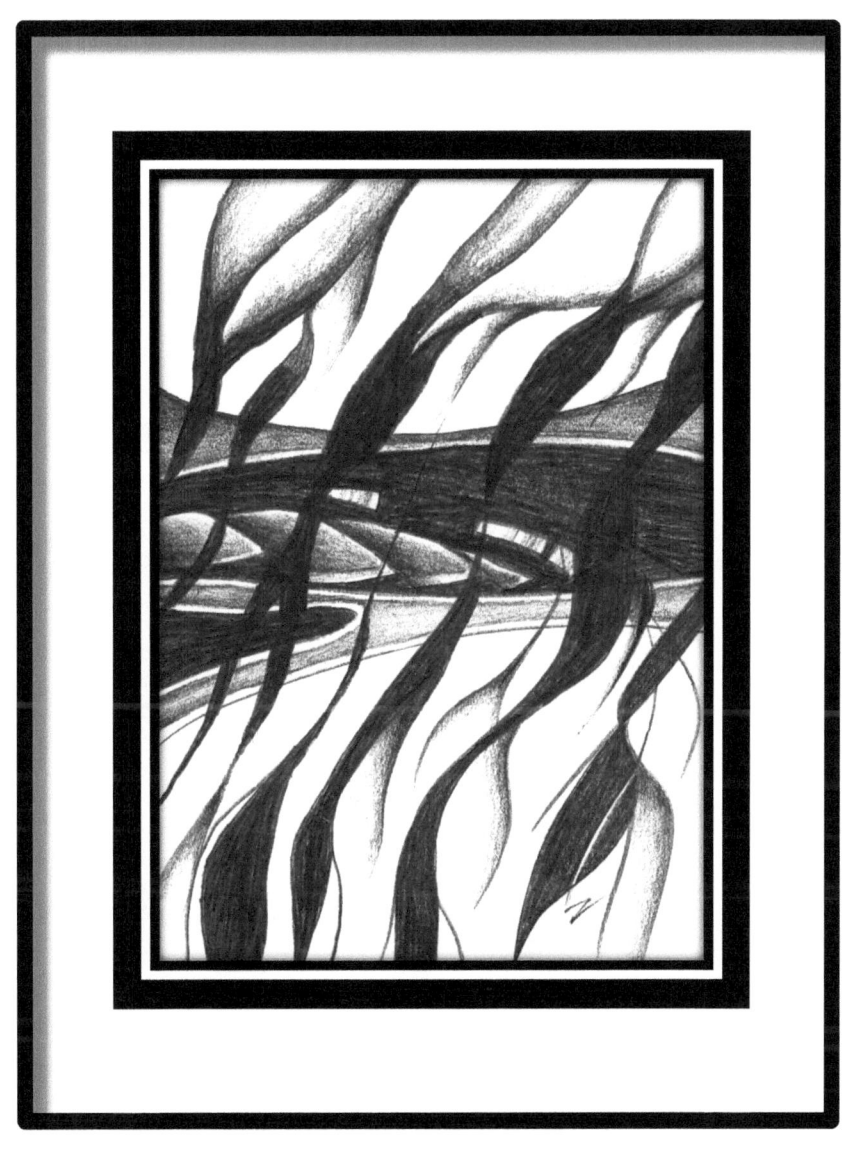

Gentle Worlds Colliding
5 x 7 pencil on paper

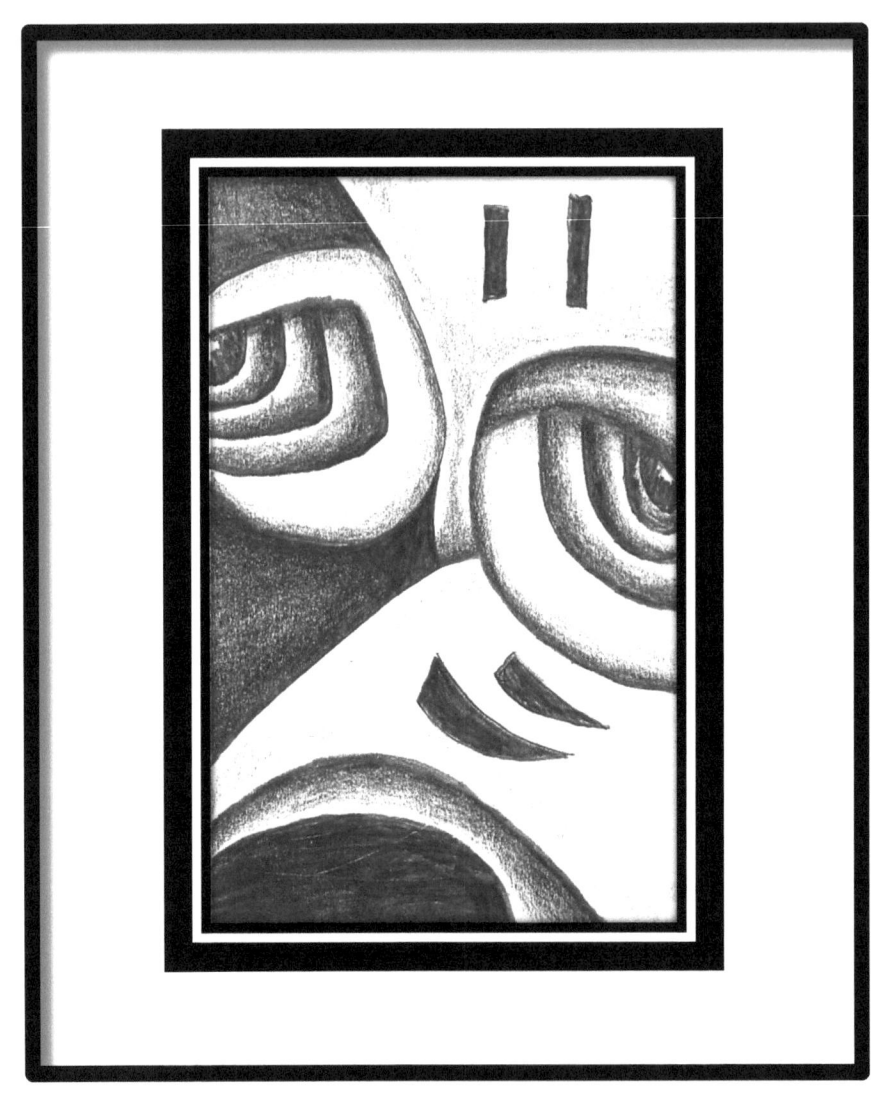

The Matador
3.5 x 5 pencil on paper

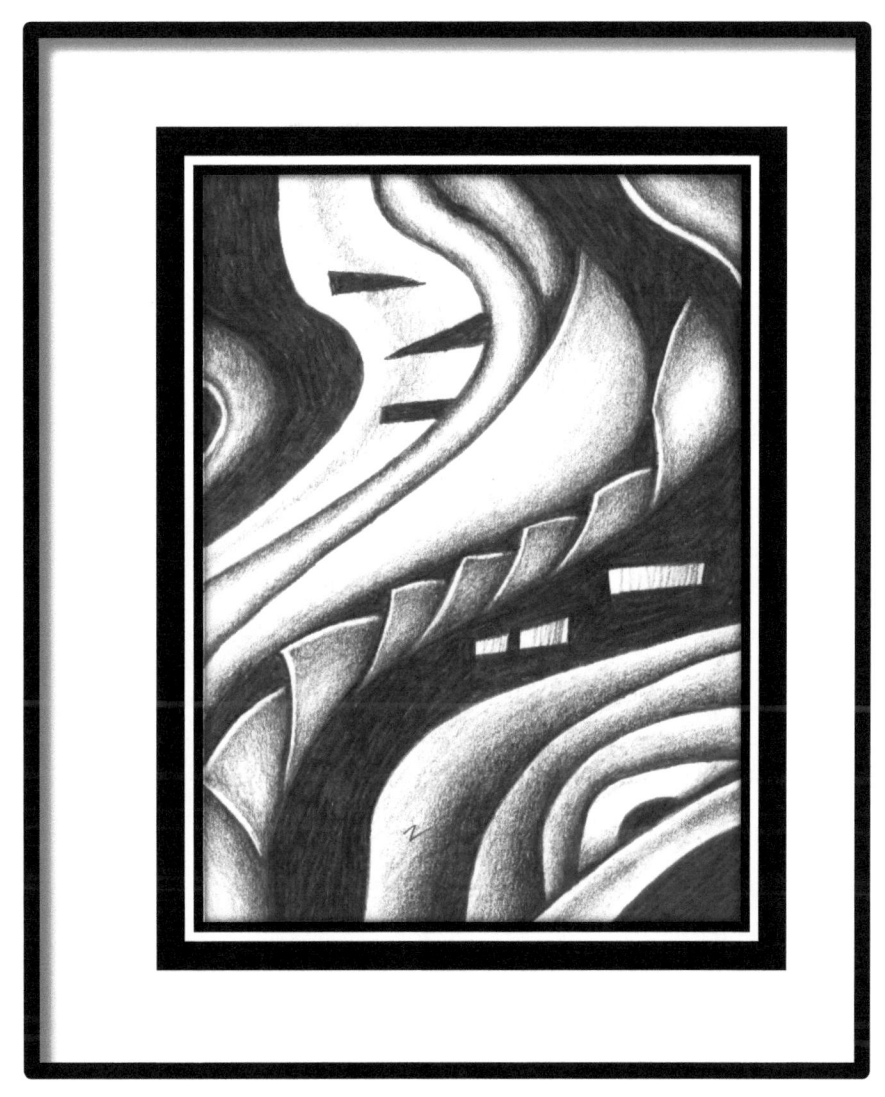

Somewhere On The Path To Andromeda
5 x 7 pencil on paper

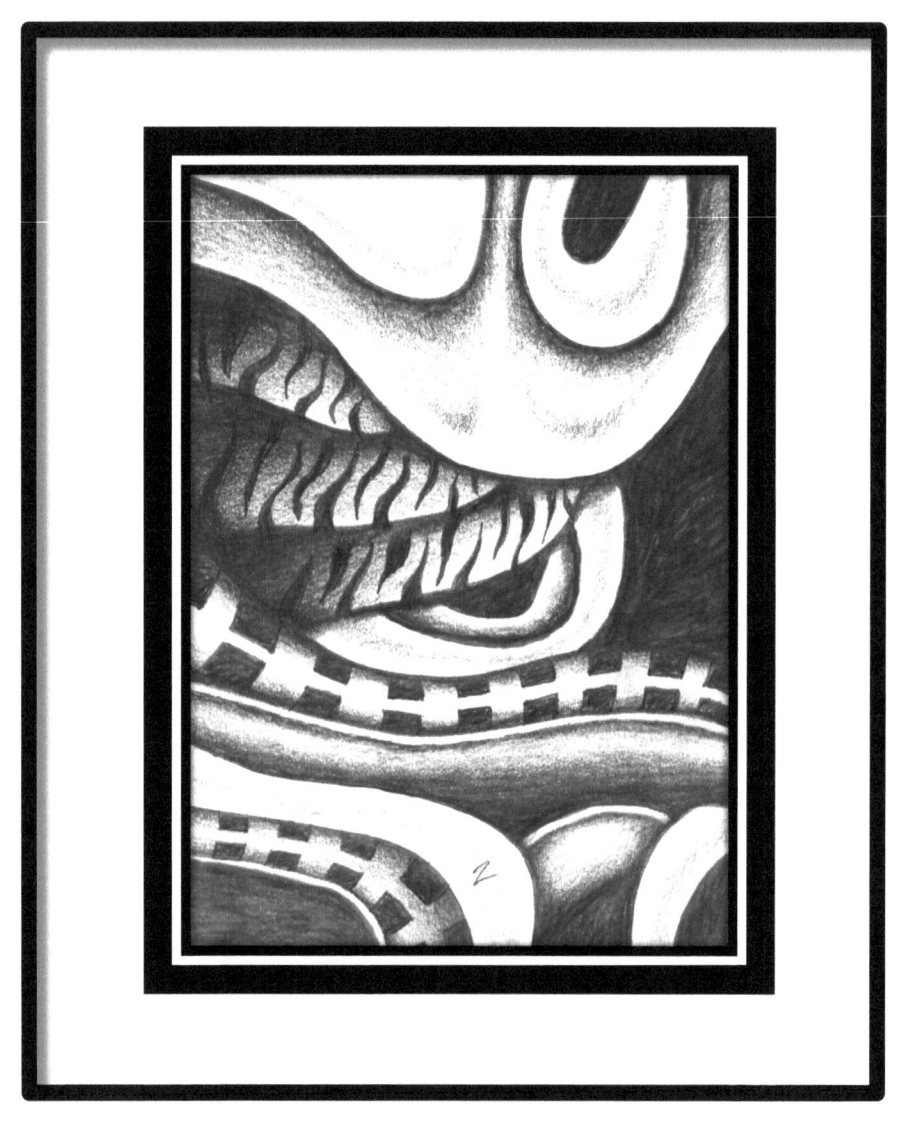

Eye Of The Tiger Path Of The Snake
5 x 7 pencil on paper

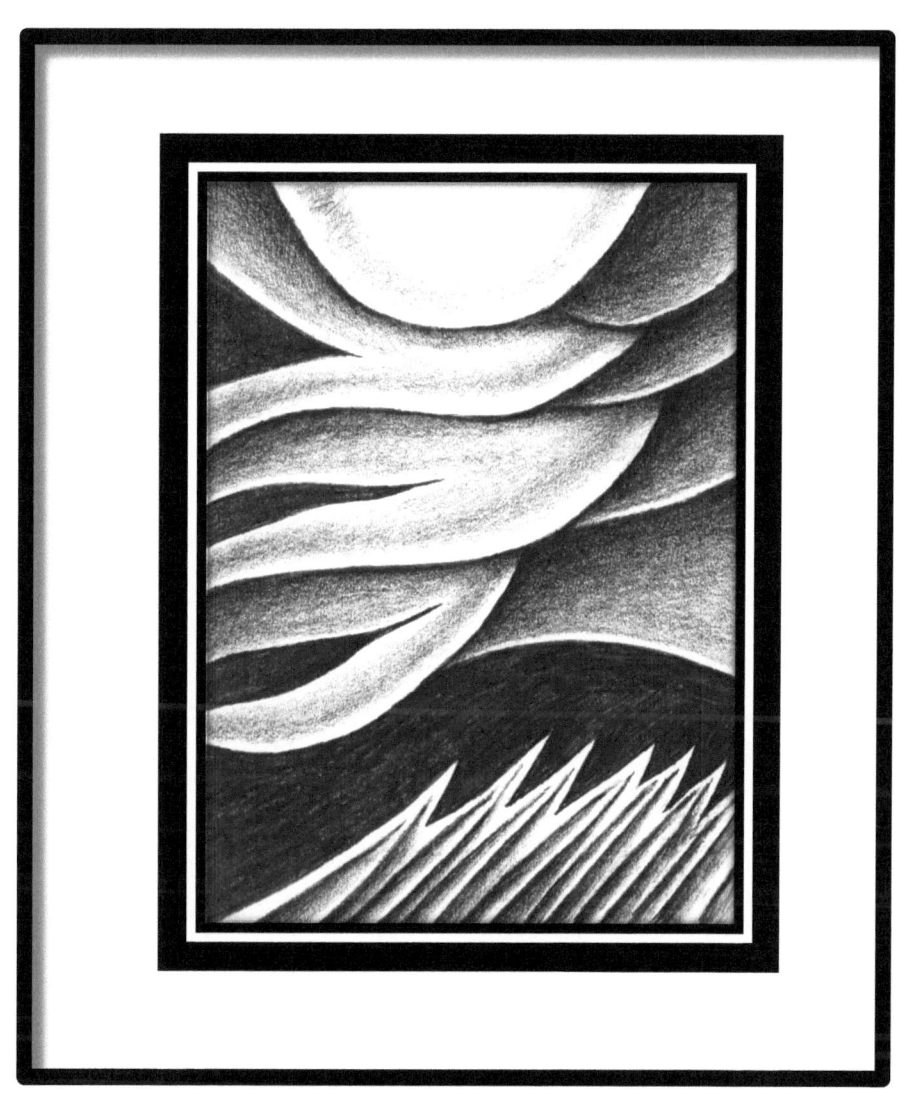

Werewolf Moon
5 x 7 pencil on paper

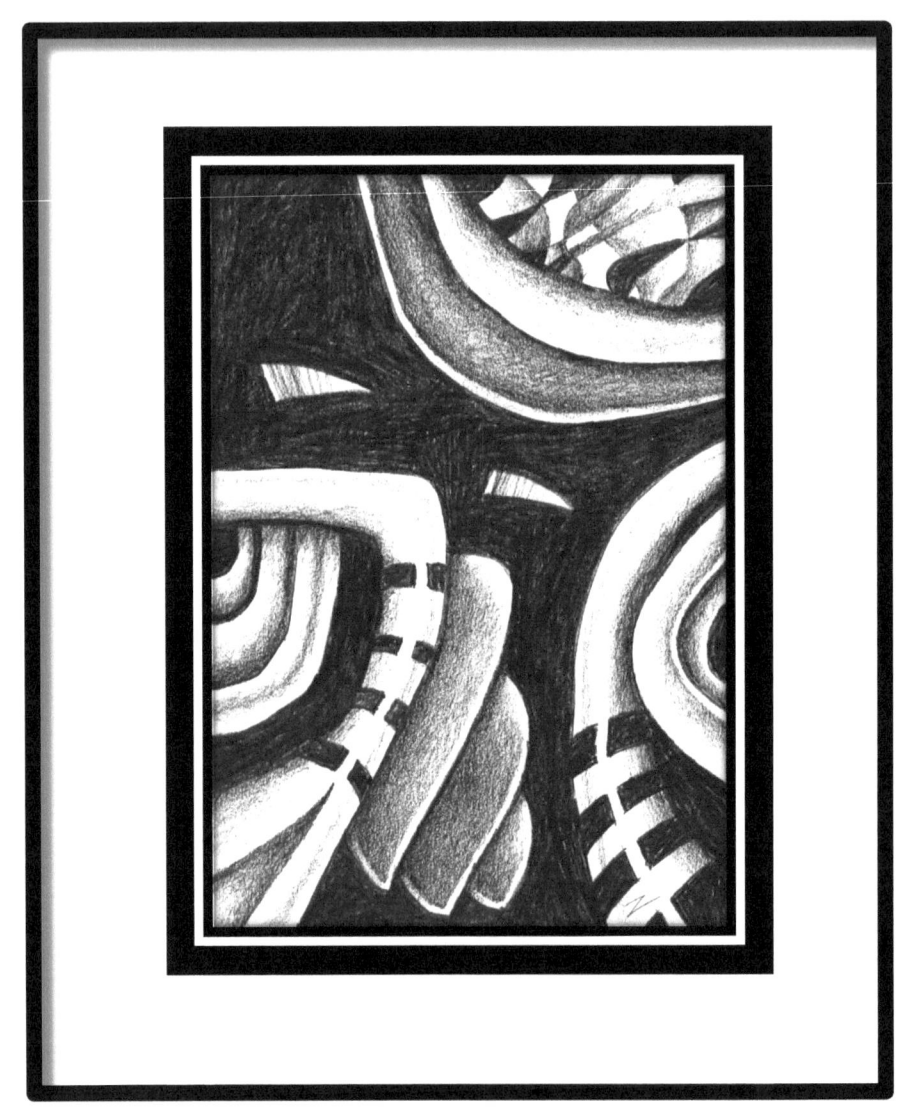

Two Clowns
5 x 7 pencil on paper

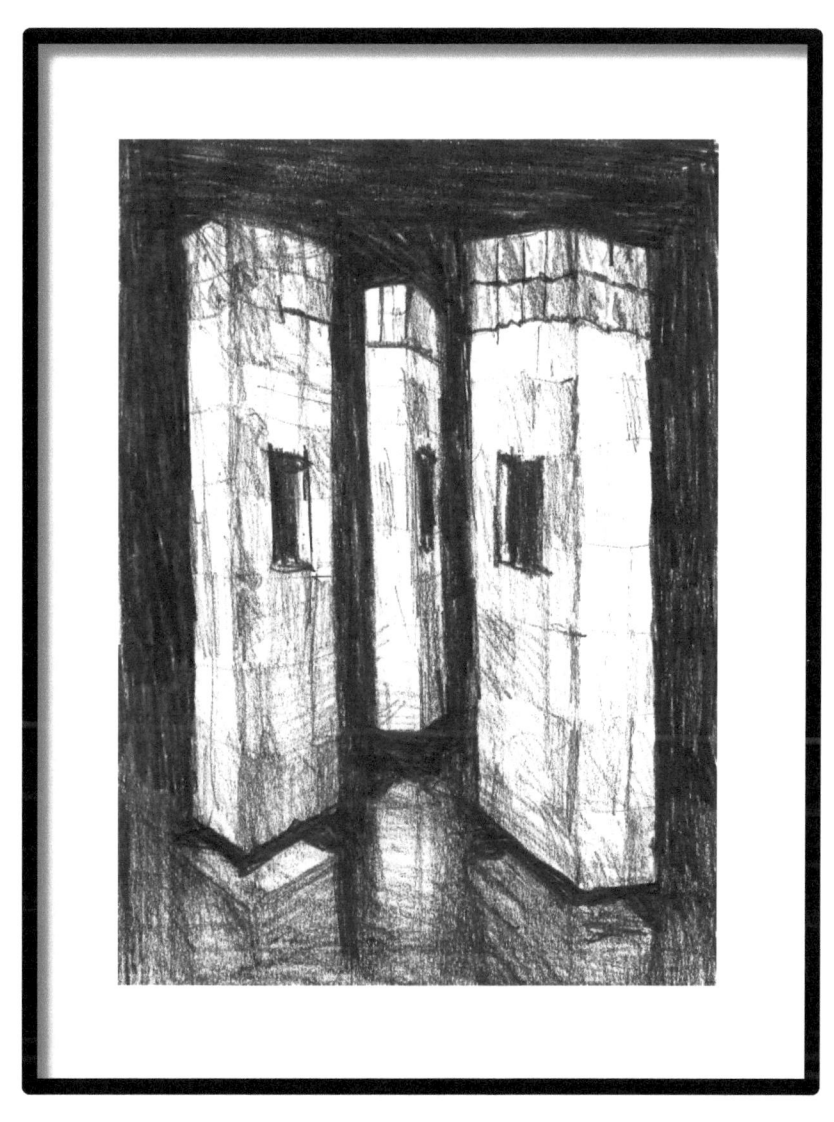

Three Floating Monuments (study)
6 x 10 pencil

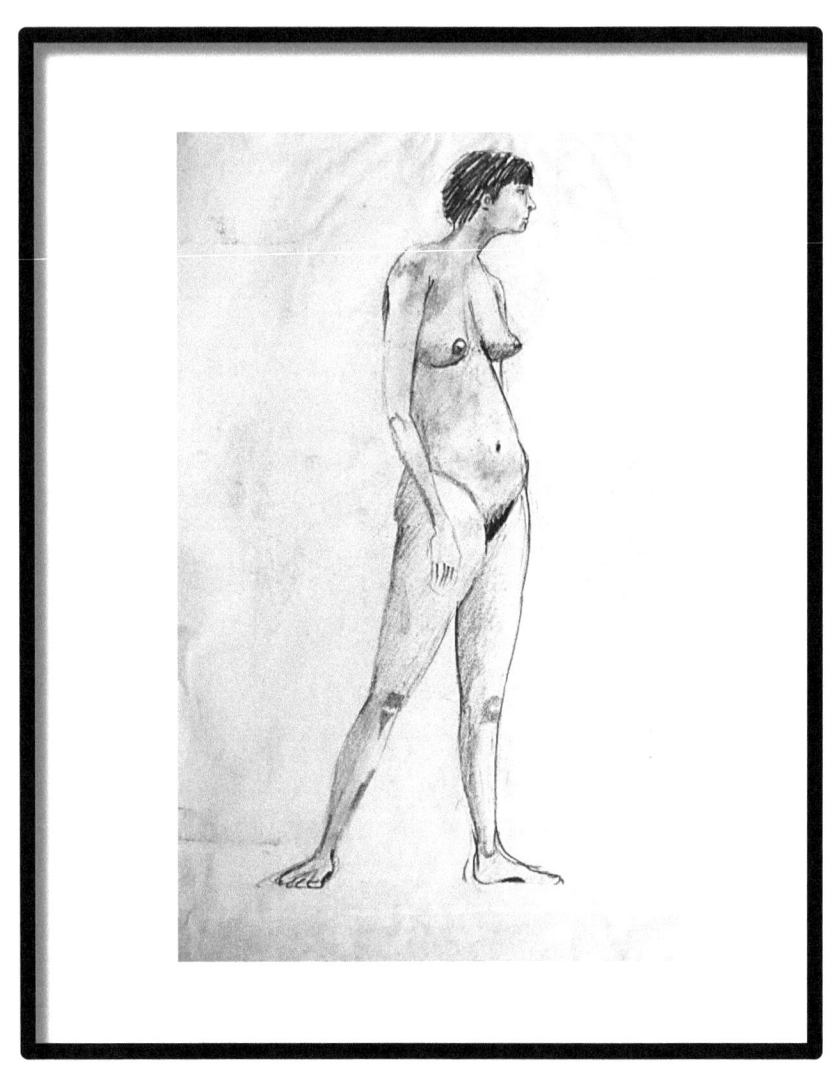

What Is Sausha Thinking #1
20 x 30 pencil on paper

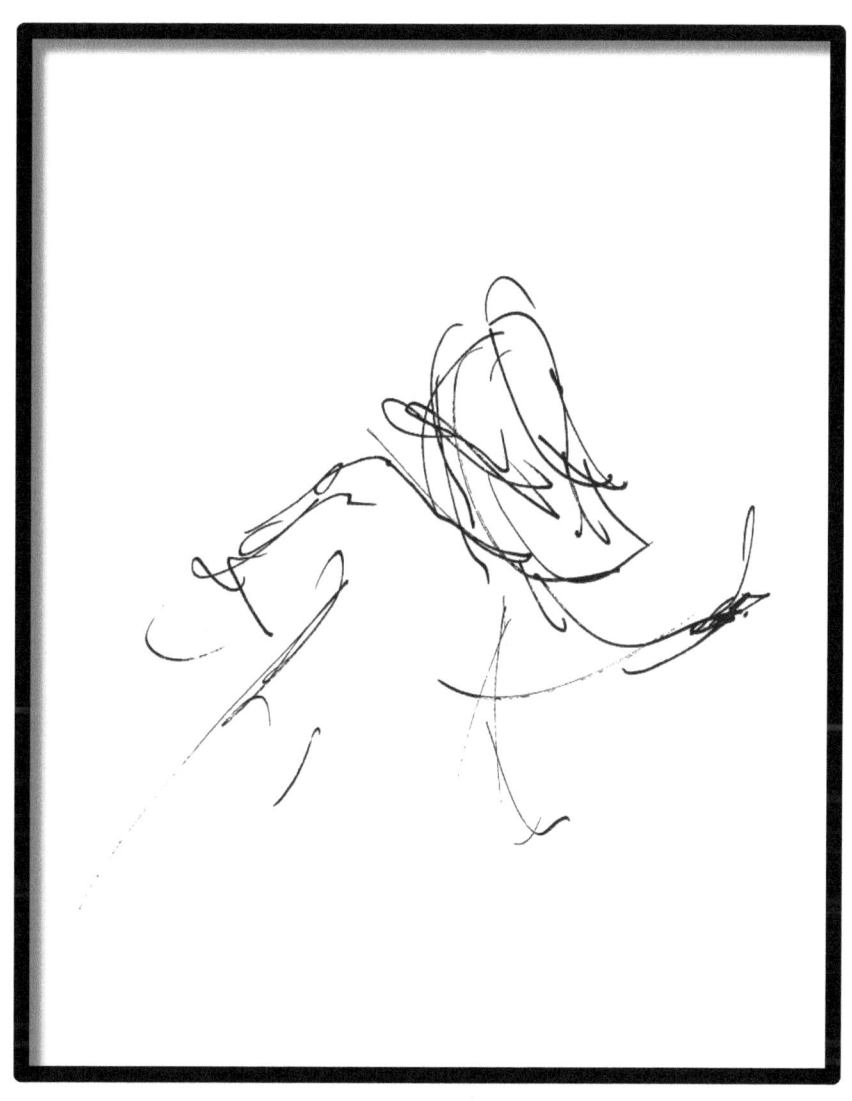

Woman dancing at a Mumbo Gumbo concert in Roseville, CA - 9/14/14 - sharpie on paper

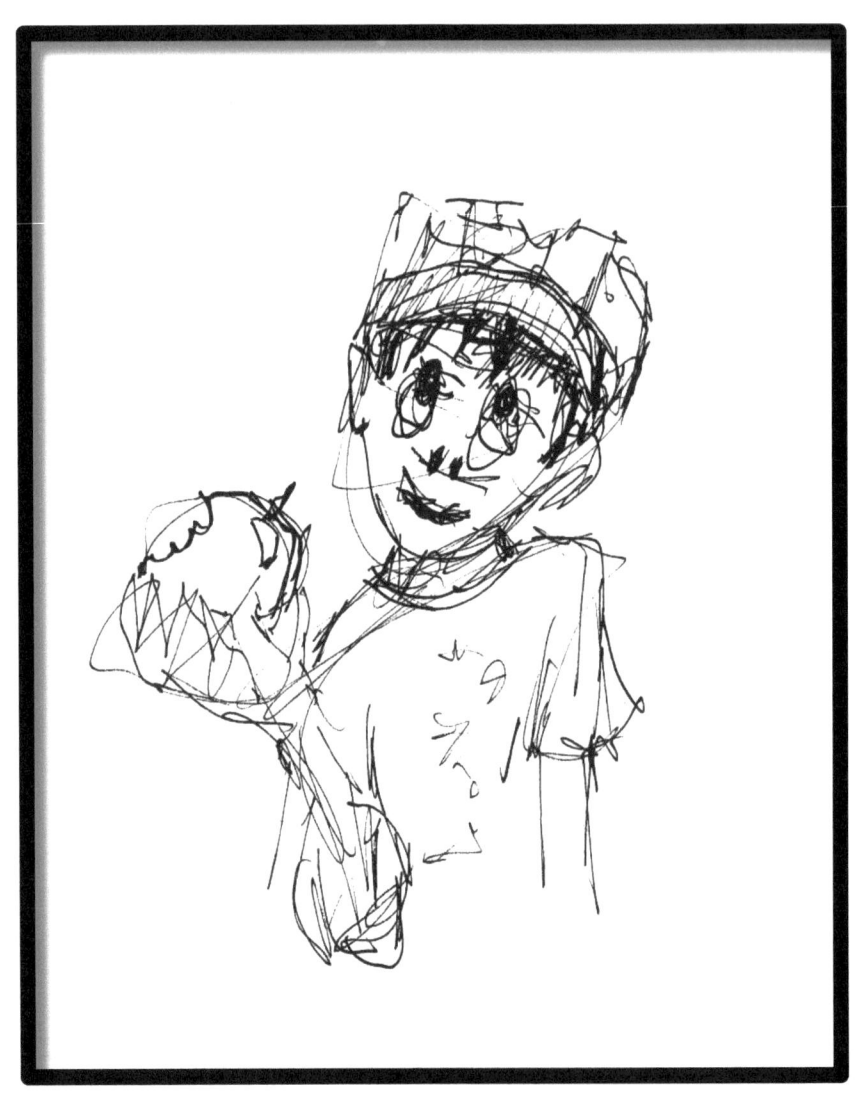

The Apple Eater
Sharpie on paper

ARCHITECTURE
Concepts

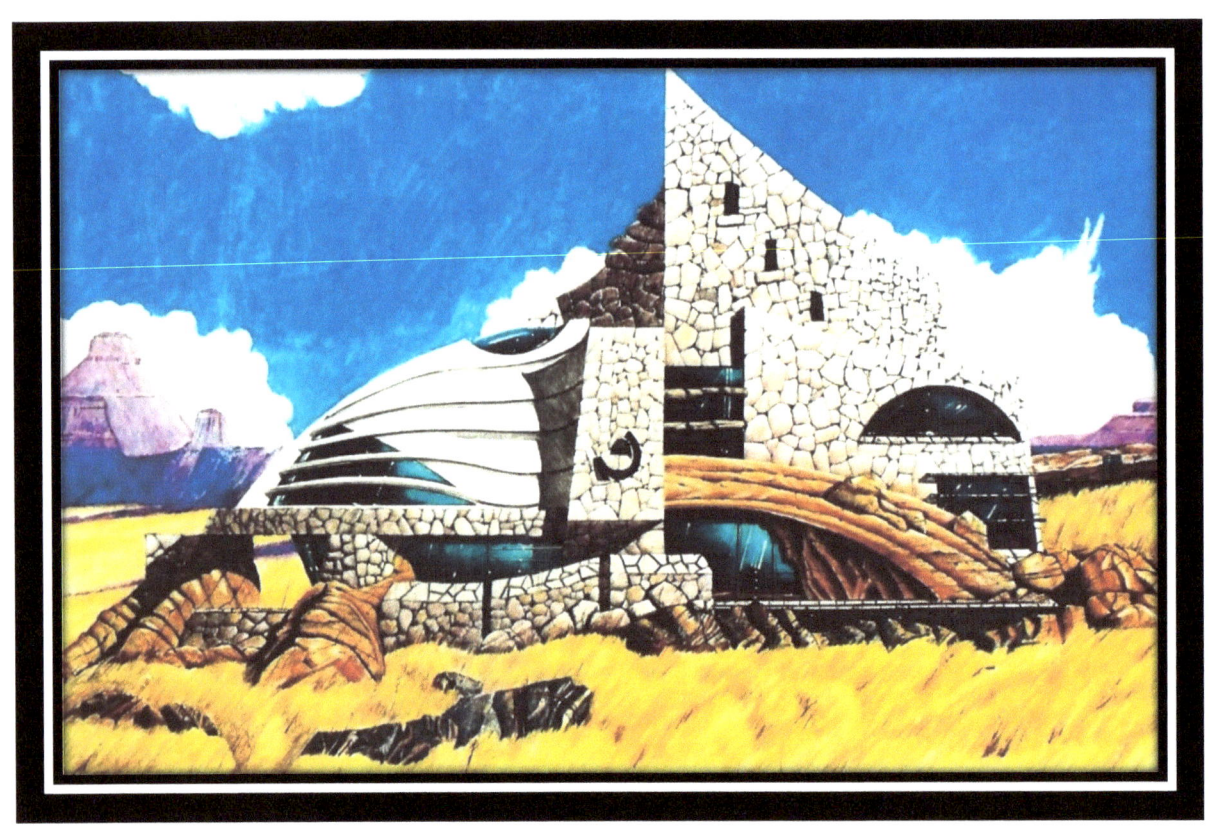

BANDOLE

Gypsy Dancer - 1992

5,360 s.f.

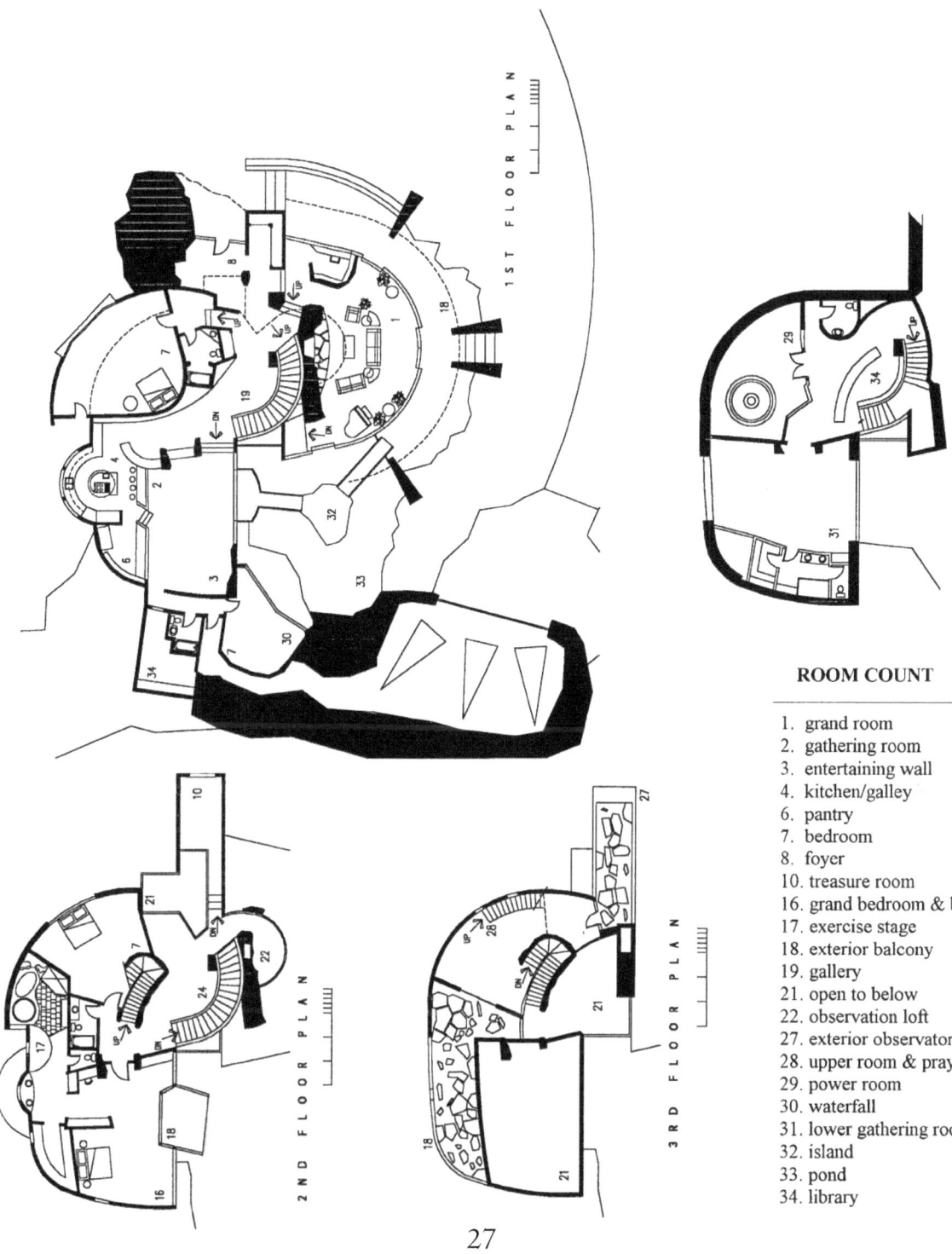

ROOM COUNT

1. grand room
2. gathering room
3. entertaining wall
4. kitchen/galley
6. pantry
7. bedroom
8. foyer
10. treasure room
16. grand bedroom & bath
17. exercise stage
18. exterior balcony
19. gallery
21. open to below
22. observation loft
27. exterior observatory
28. upper room & prayer tower
29. power room
30. waterfall
31. lower gathering room
32. island
33. pond
34. library

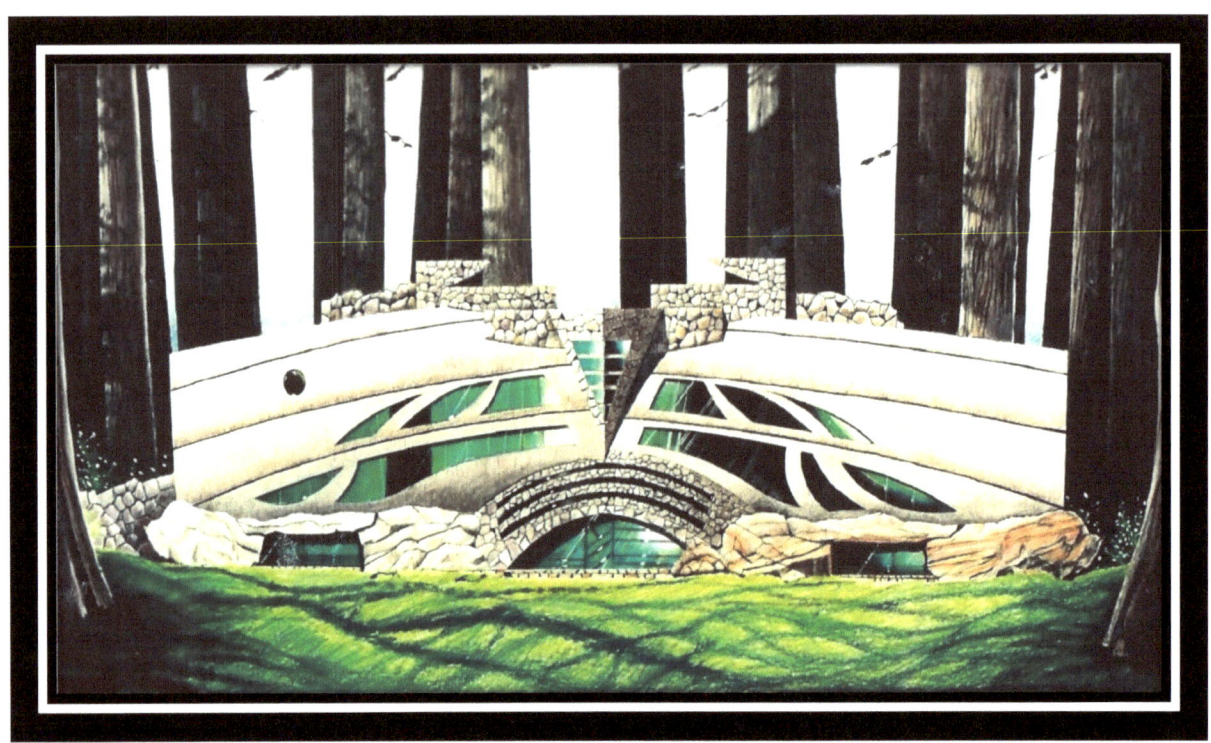

BOREALIS

House of The North Wind - 1992

12,260 s.f.

Can you find the Red and White buffalo in the picture?

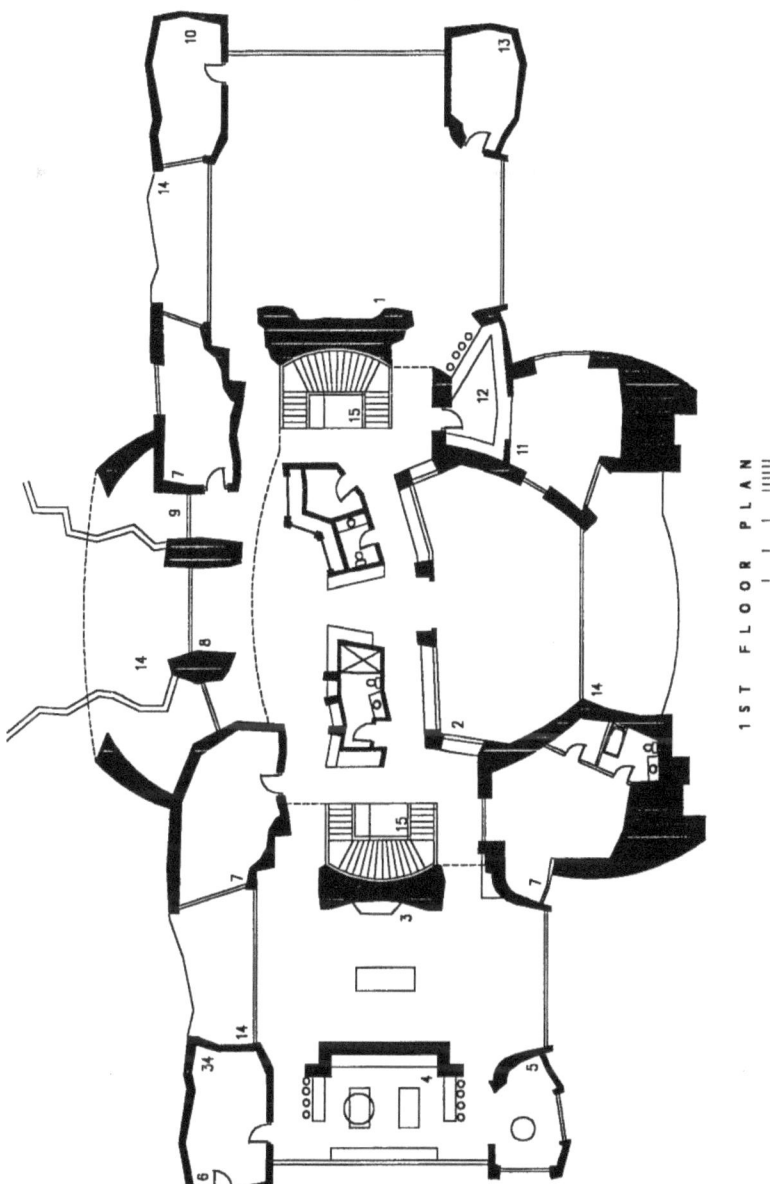

ROOM COUNT

1. grand room
2. gathering room
3. entertaining hall
4. kitchen/galley
5. nook
6. office
7. bedroom
8. foyer
9. window garden
10. study
11. garden room
12. bar
13. storage
14. exterior patio
15. elevator
16. grand bedroom & bath
17. exercise
18. upper patio
19. upper gallery
20. grand suites
21. open to below
22. observatory
34. pantry

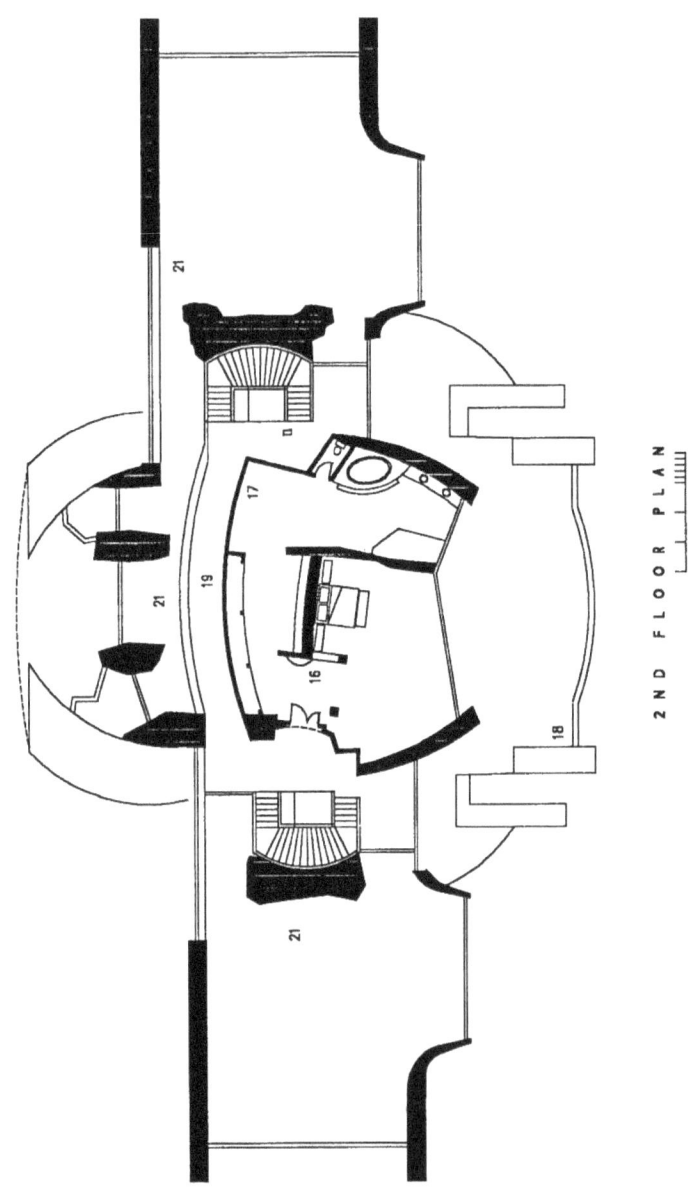

2ND FLOOR PLAN

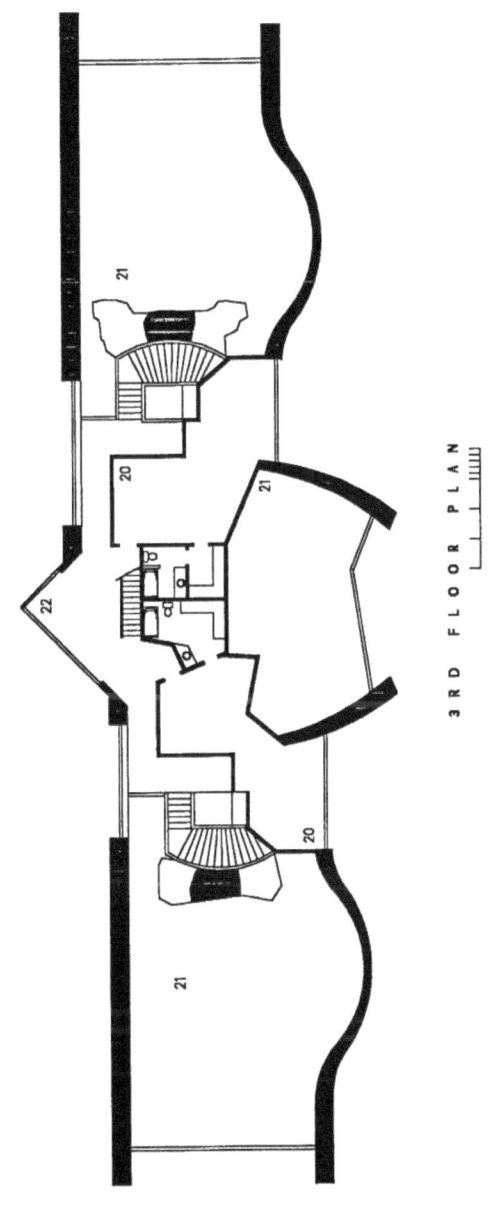

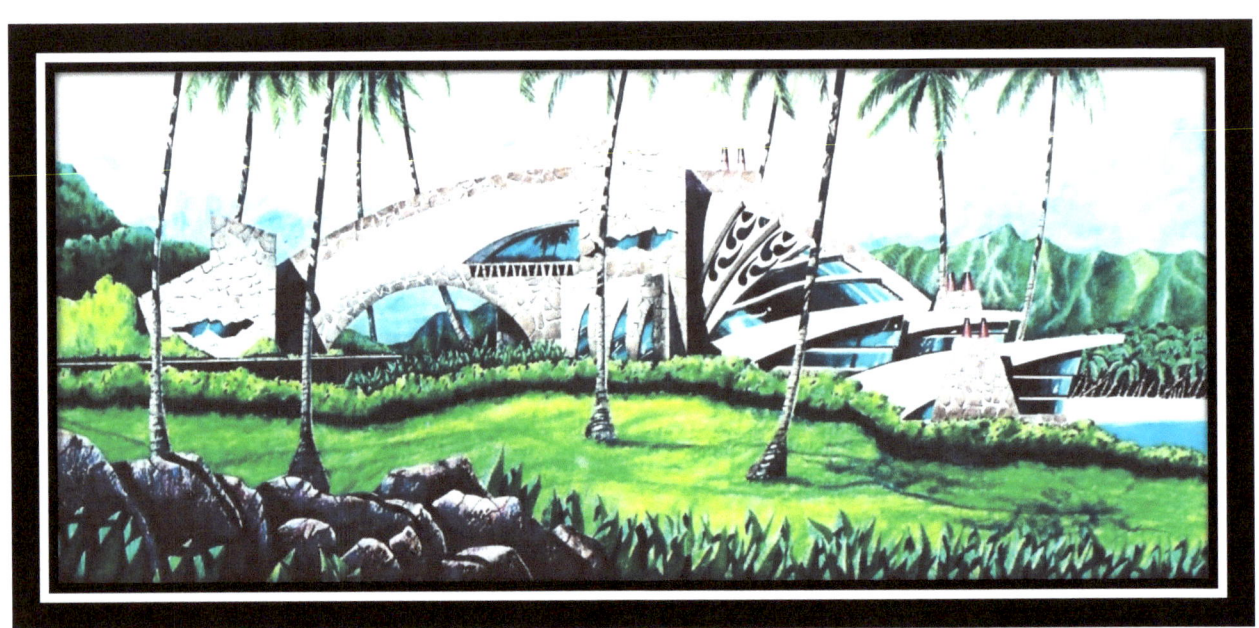

CHERI ZAHN

Place of Brilliance - 1994

12,060 s.f.

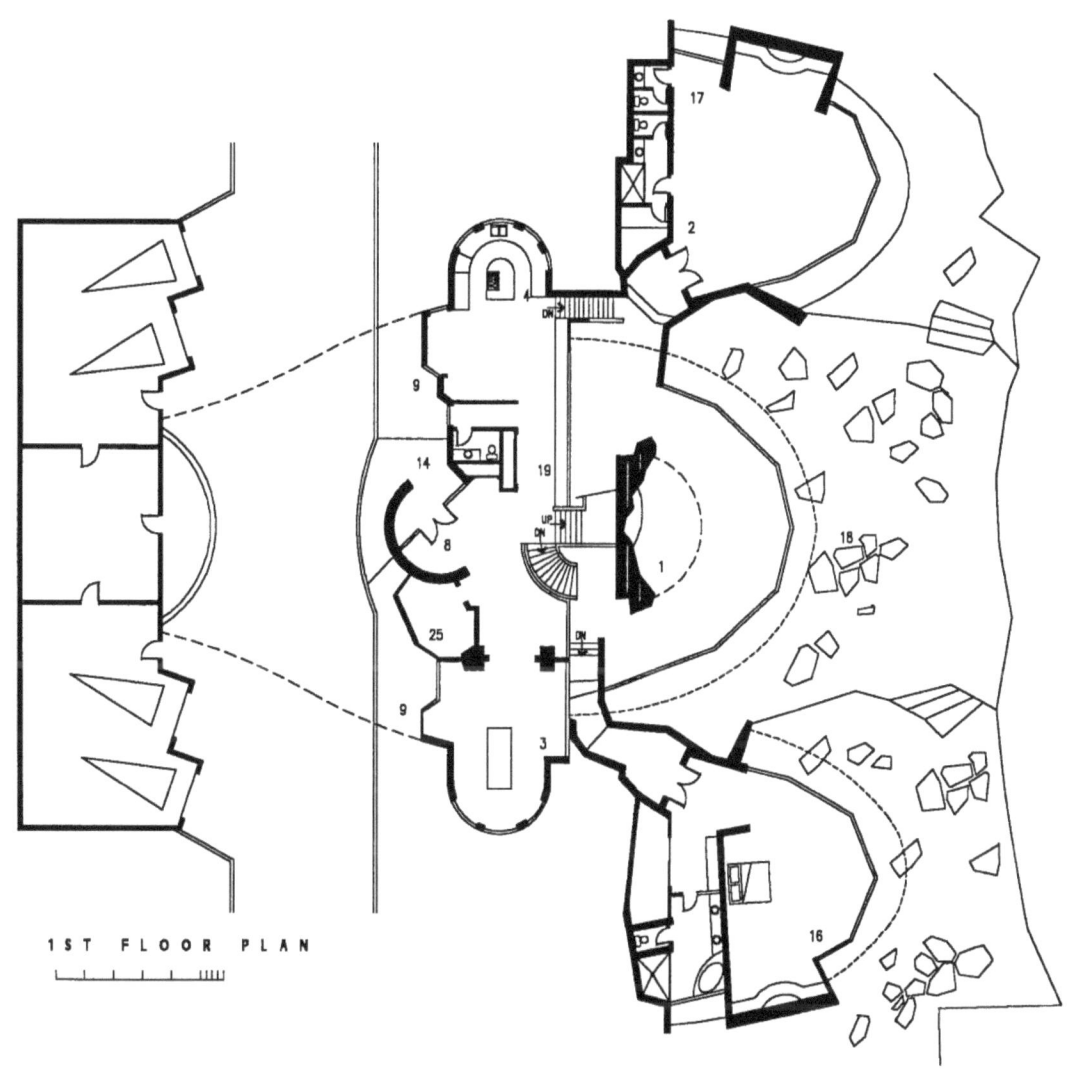

1ST FLOOR PLAN

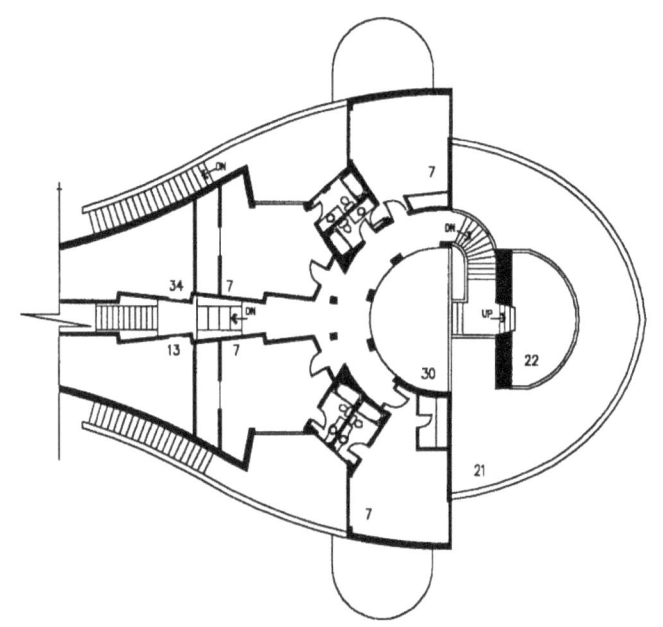

2ND FLOOR PLAN

ROOM COUNT

1. livingroom & gallery
2. sauna
3. dining
4. kitchen/galley
7. bedrooms
8. foyer
9. window garden
13. storage
14. exterior foyer
16. east bedroom
17. west bedroom
19. gallery
21. open to below
22. observation loft
25. treasure room
30. upper gathering
34. storage

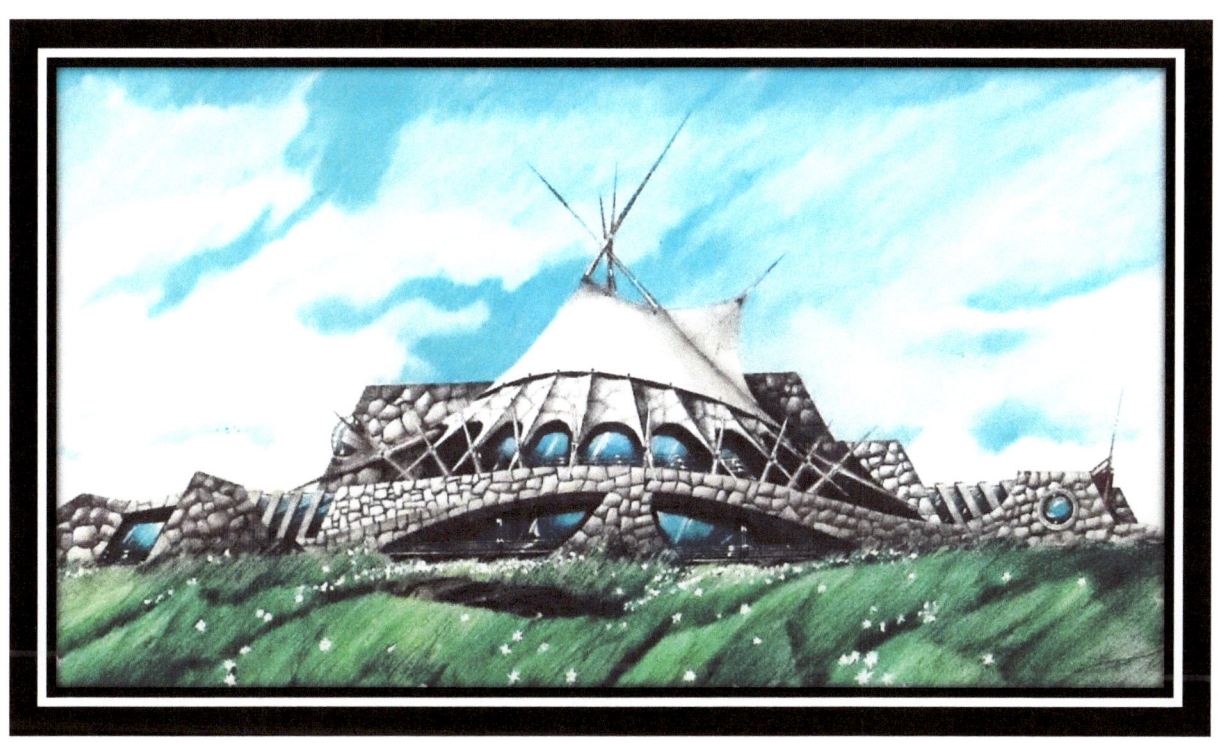

APACHIE RISE

17,578 s.f. - 1993

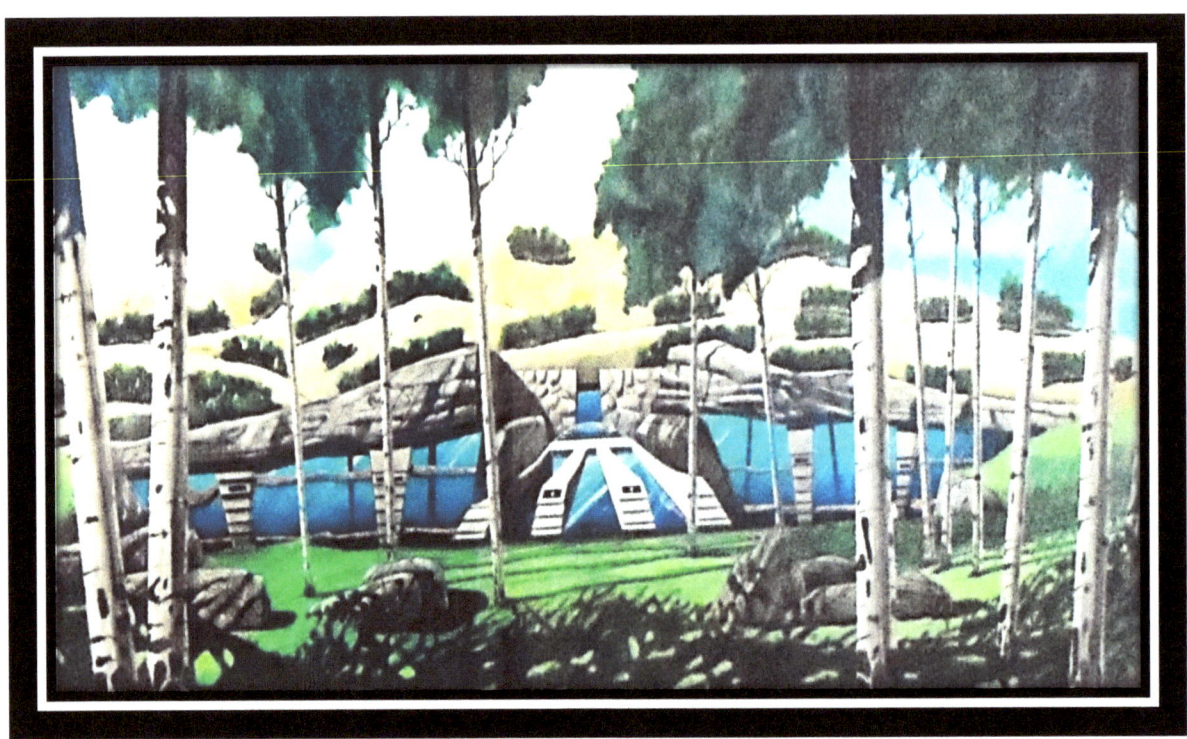

GAILMORA

6,270 s.f. - 1993

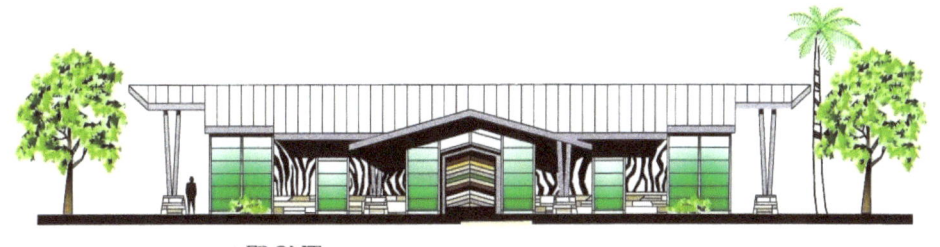

FRONT ELEVATION

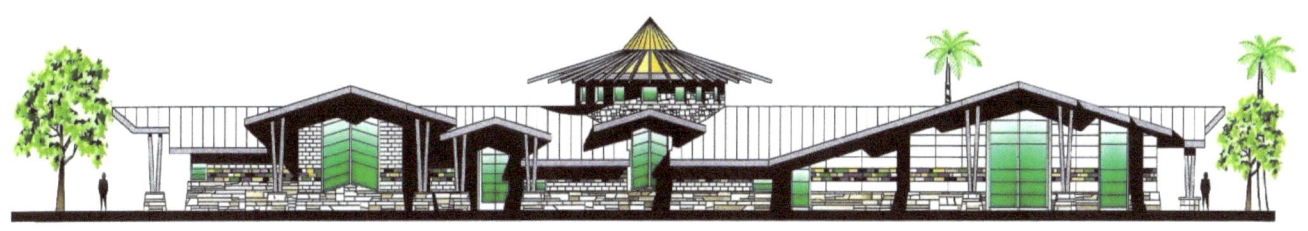

LEFT SIDE ELEVATION COLOR STYLE 1 COLOR STYLE 2

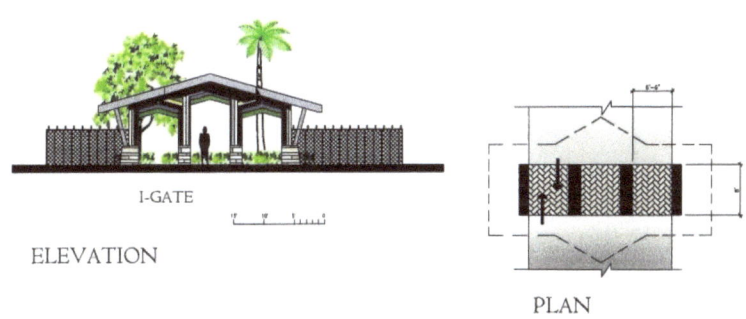

I-GATE ELEVATION

PLAN

School For Peace & Hope

Nigeria, Africa - 2013

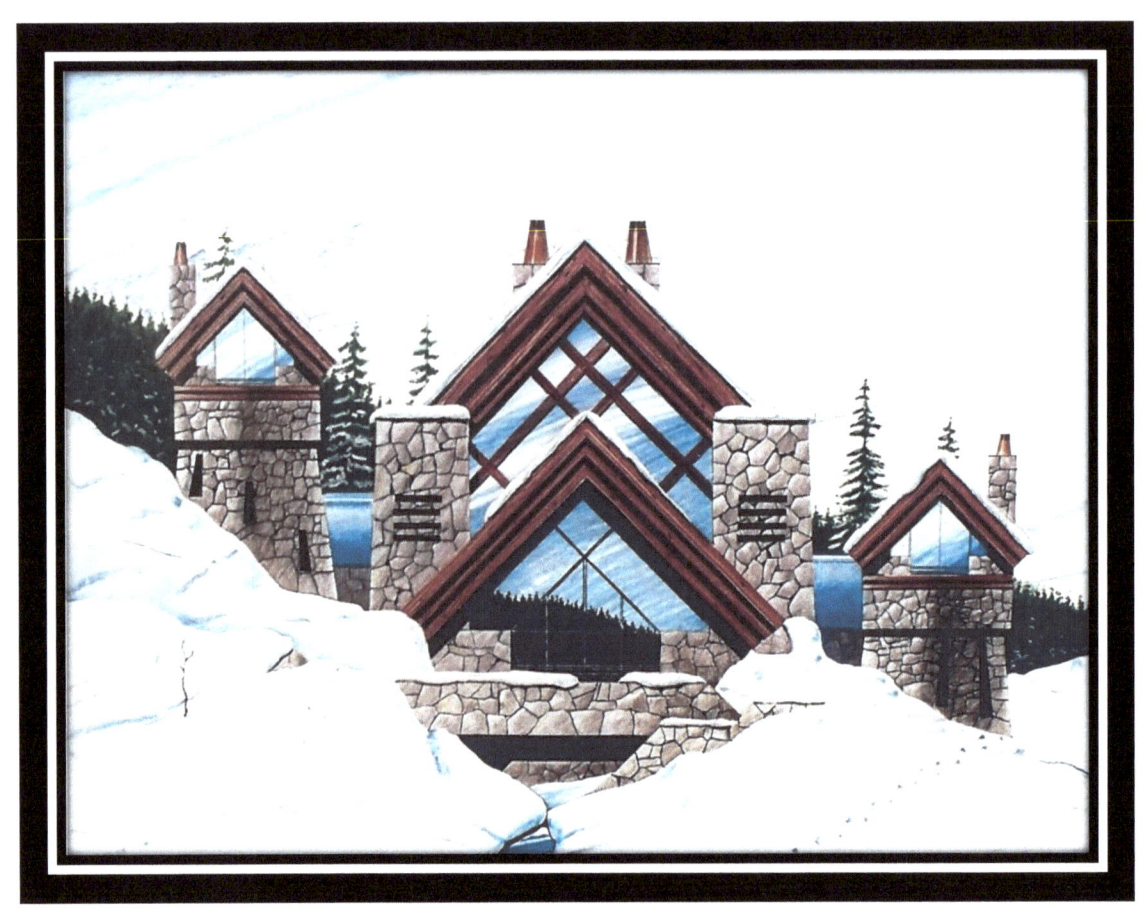

REDSTONE

7,560 s.f. - 1993

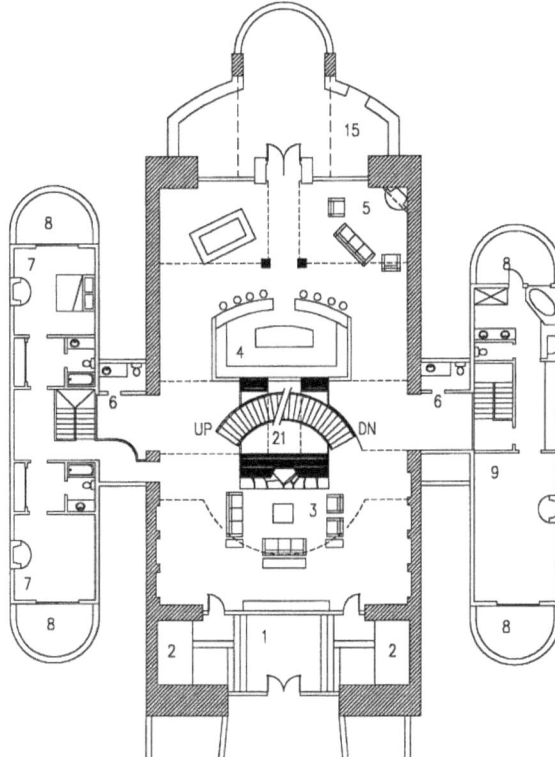

MAIN FLOOR PLAN

ROOM COUNT

1. foyer
2. closets and ski storage
3. livingroom & gallery
4. kitchen/galley
5. gathering room
6. powder room
7. bedrooms
8. exterior balcony
9. grand bedroom & bath
10. open to below
11. conversation loft
12. bunk loft
13. basement
15. exterior patio

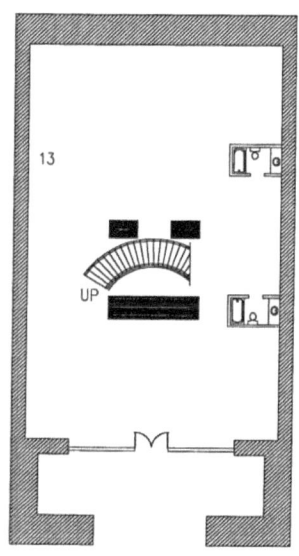

LOWER FLOOR PLAN

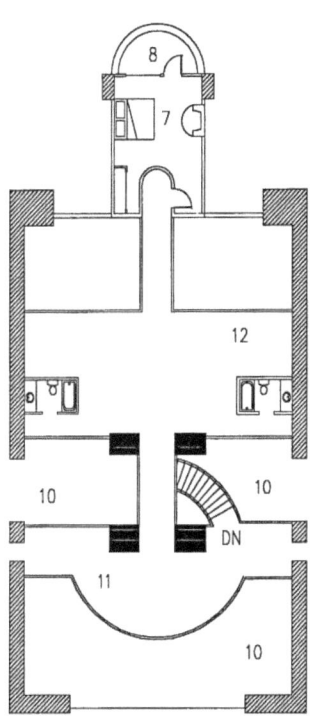

UPPER FLOOR PLAN

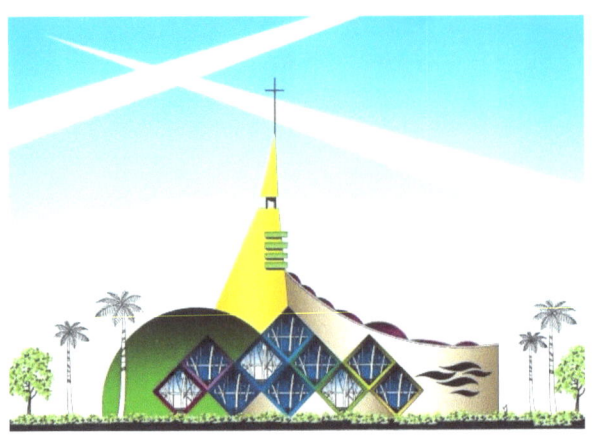

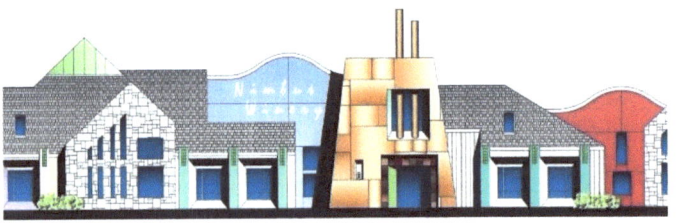

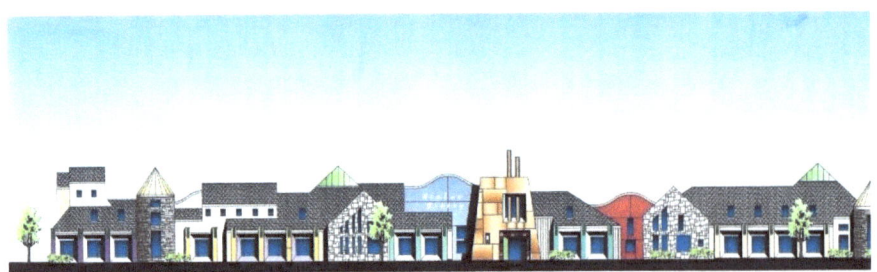

Nimbus Winery & Church

Conceptual - 1998

ARCHITECTURE

New Visions

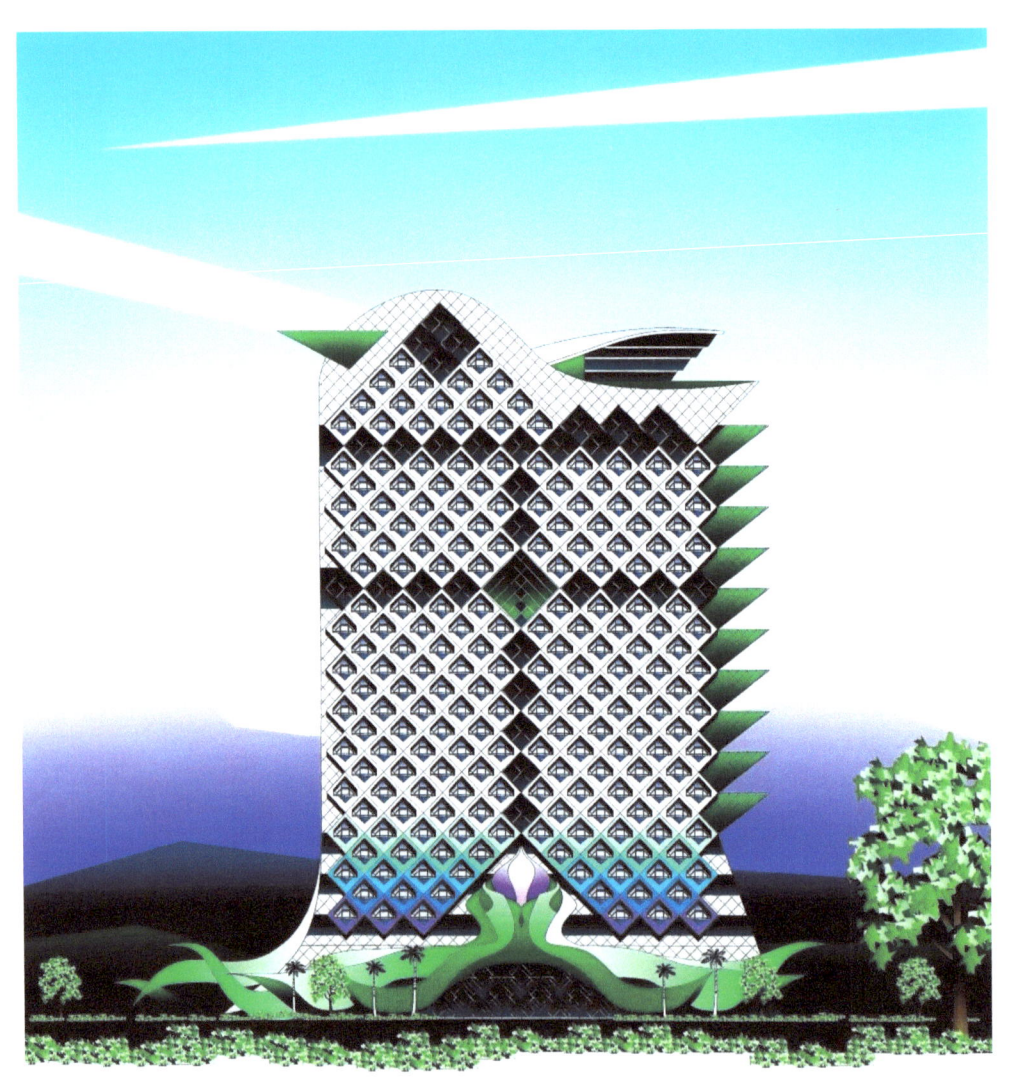

Shamrock Falls - *2007*

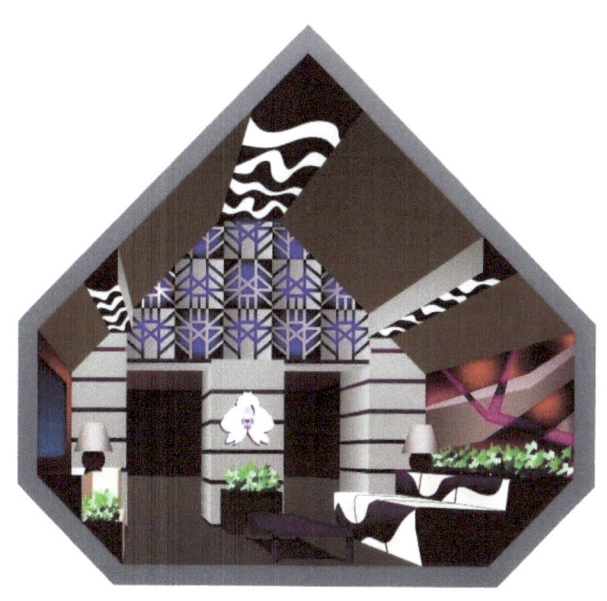

Living Room

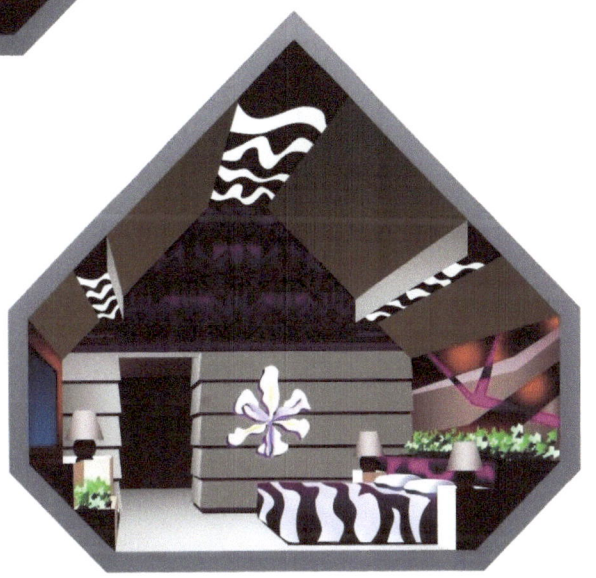

Bed Room

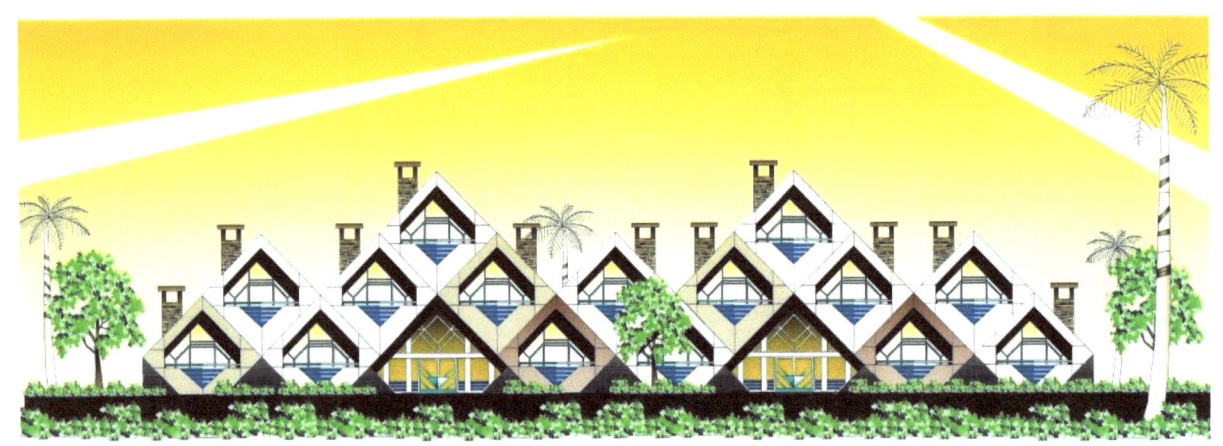

Sunset Shores

Resort - 2007

POETRY

Illustrated

2010 - 2018

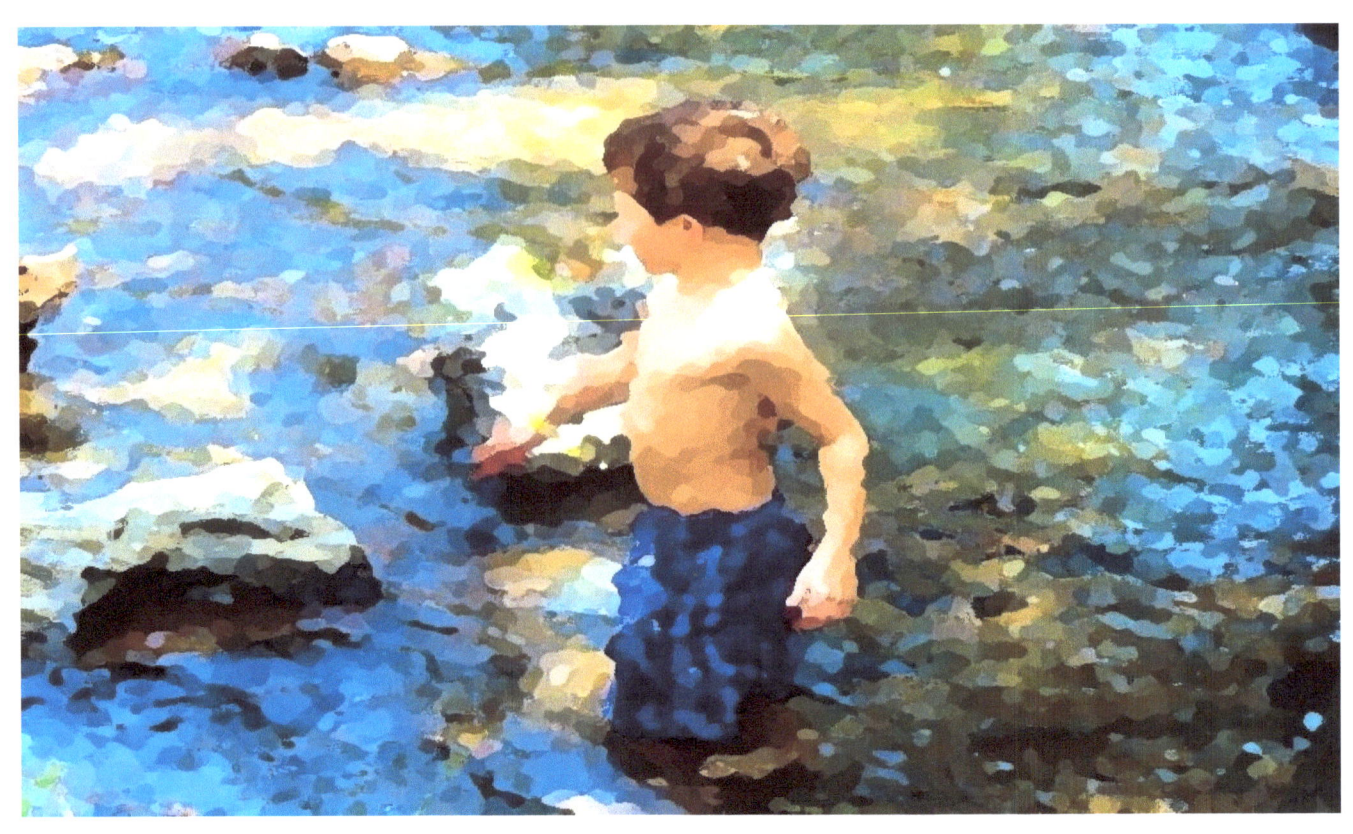

Into The Future

I can gaze into the future
And peer into the past
And I know that what I gaze upon
Is destined not to last

So as I leave today
And start in towards tomorrow
May my touch provide much joy
And avoid the sting of sorrow

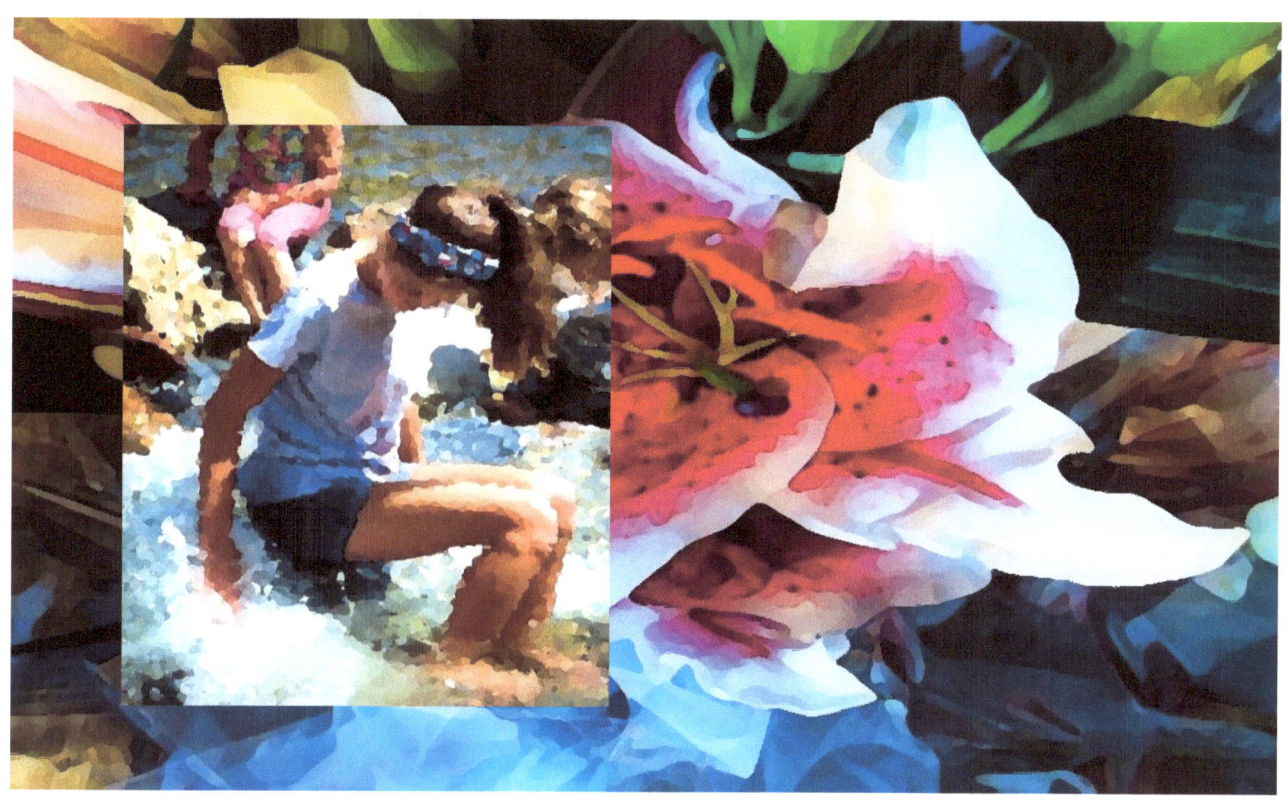

Protesting

The seasons are creeping
Time makes its demand
And no matter your stance
And no matter your stand

The race will end
No matter your route
And it will not matter
The raise of your shout

For to protest the aging
The passing of years
Time does not listen
For it has no ears

Fishing

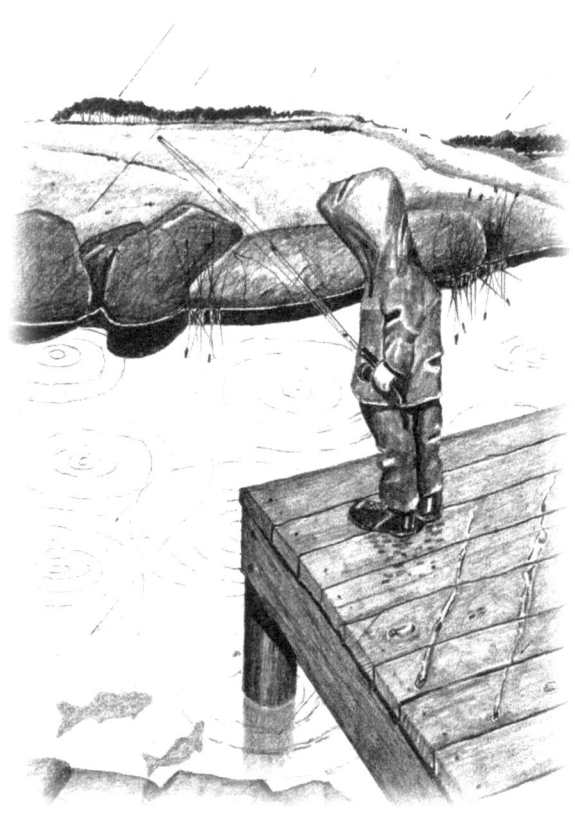

I went fishing today,
And it started to rain.
There were ripples on the pond,
I thought would scare the fish away.

But, I peeked over the edge,
And saw fish swimming about.
They were gliding through the water,
Just weaving in and out.

I watched them for a while,
How peaceful they all looked.
So, I just stood there very still.
I didn't even bait my hook.

Waterfall

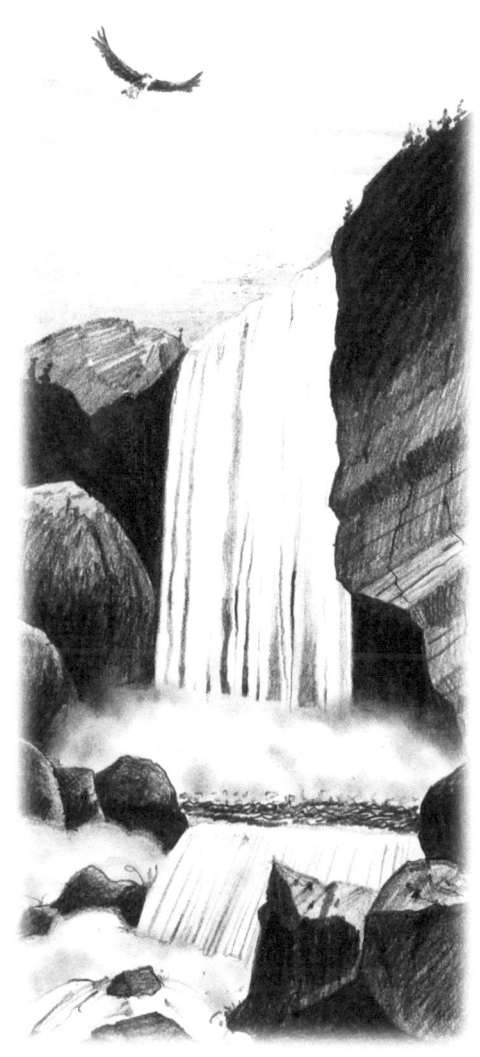

(A boy talks to the waterfall)

Oh, Waterfall,
Waterfall,
How majestic is your view,

How tall you are,
How far you fall.
Does anyone care for you?

. . . .

(The Waterfall answers)

Yes, my friend,
Oh, my friend.
There is someone close by.

Near they are,
And care they do.
I'm watched with an eagle eye.

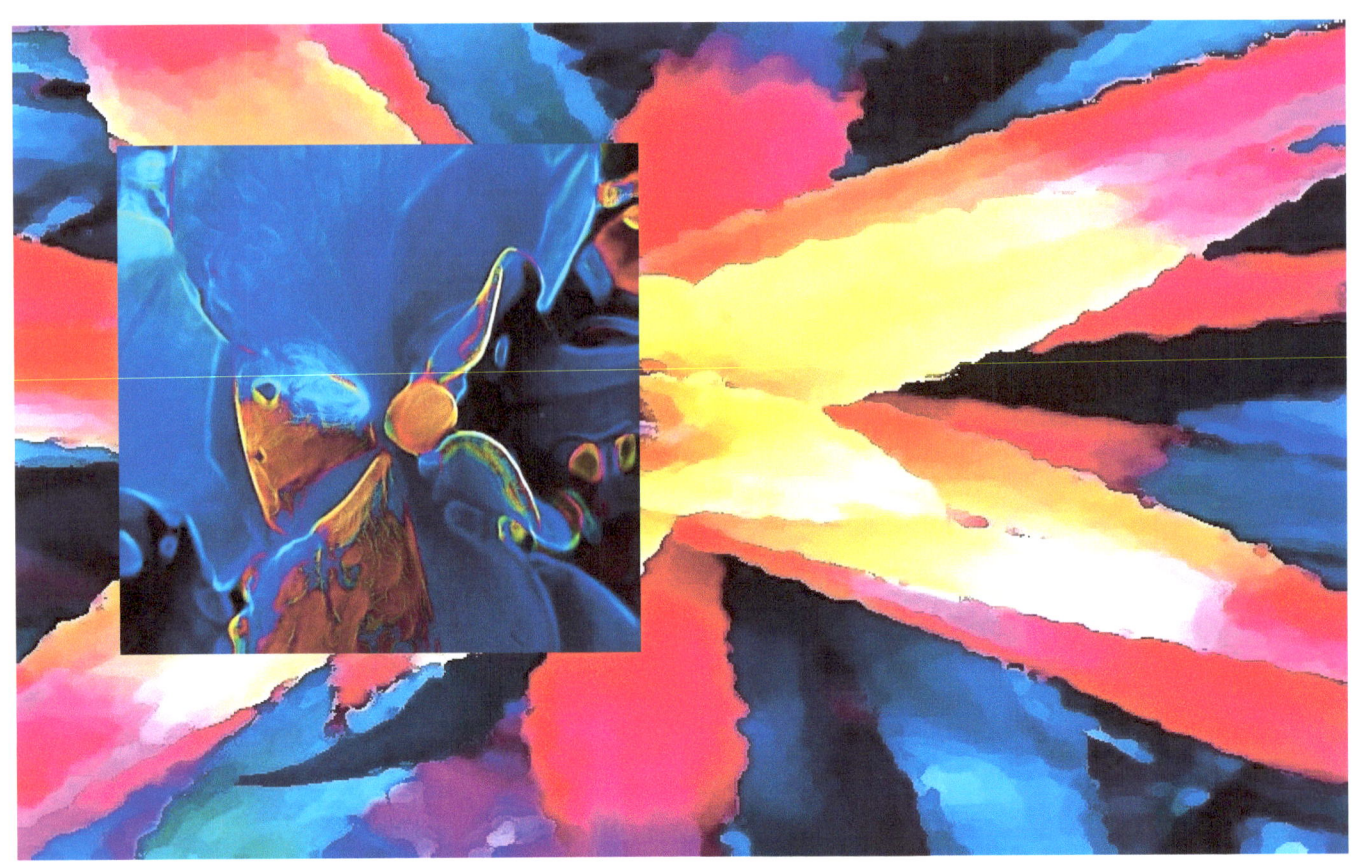

Into The Wild

I hungered to discover
What I did not know
So I ventured into the wild

My ticket well bought
My fate well set
Its wonders set me Beguiled

So the course I drew
With wondered resolve
The past was now reviled

As I hungered to discover
What I did not know
So I ventured into the wild

A Fork In The Road

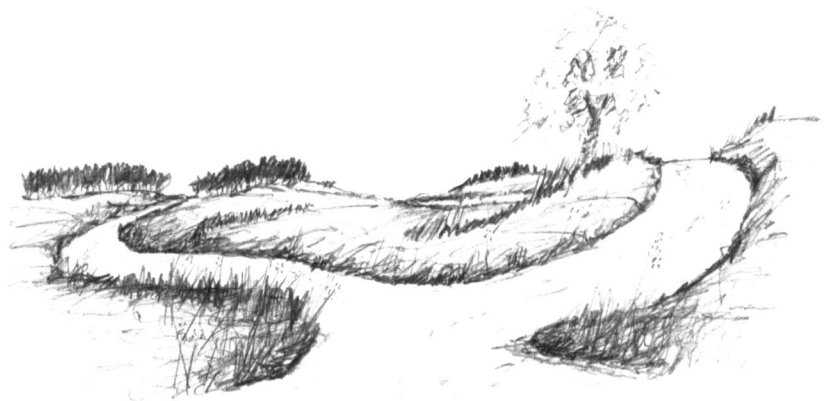

I came to a fork in the road,
And didn't know which to take.
So I quietly sat down and pondered,
'Which choice was I to make'?

I thought for quite a while,
And wrestled with my thoughts.
And wondered, "What if I chose wrong?
Just what would be the costs?"

"My life could change forever,
Depending upon my choice.
One could lead to fortunes,
And one could silence my voice."

So I stood in much reflection
And peered to each extreme
Knowing the choice that laid before me
Was tougher than it did seem.

Then the wisdom of my Father
Came softly once again
When he said, "Son, (Daughter) you . . .
. . . can only choose which way to go
By understanding where you've just been.

So I made my weighty decision
And did not fear my choice
For I knew, no matter which road I chose
I would always hear my father's voice.

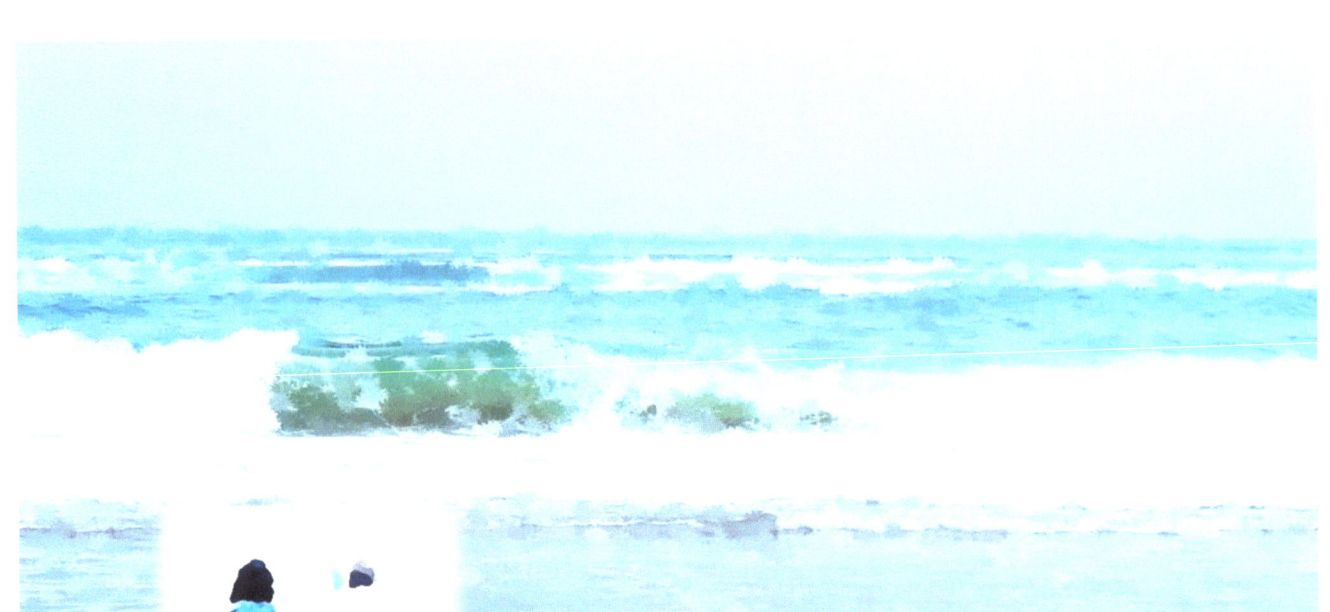

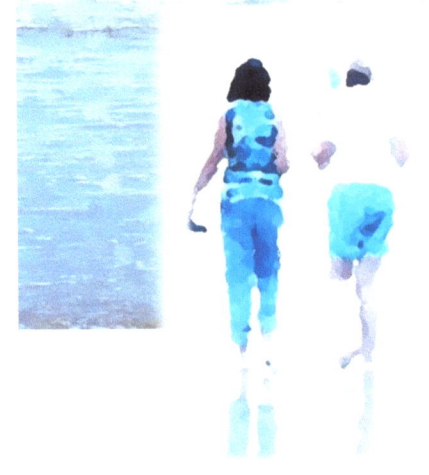

The Shore
(Stepping through the door)

I love to stick
My feet in the sand,
And walk along
This magic land.

The tides that rise
Bring renewed pleasures,
Searching high
For hidden treasures.

Worries and troubles
Fade away;
Renews my heart,
Renews my day.

It's at the shore,
Where I will be.
Join me there.
Come walk with me.

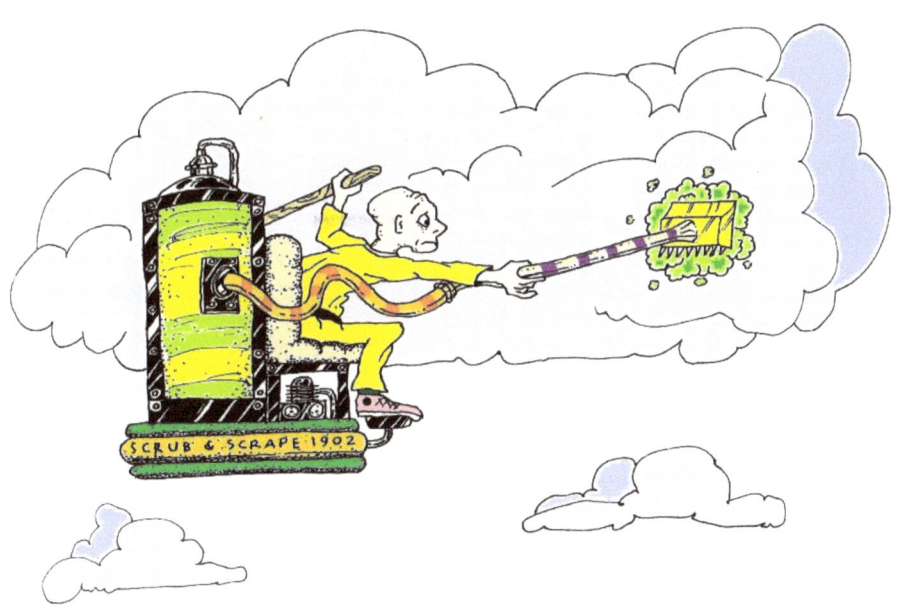

The Sky Scraper

I'm a skyscraper,
And I clean the skies,
Scrubbing the clouds
As they float by.

I take pride in my work,
And I'm good at what I do.
I've been cleaning clouds
Since 19-0-2.

But it's getting much harder
To clean off the gunk,
Because people keep making
Mountains of junk.

They make an abundance
Of doohickeys today,
They use them once,
Then throw them away.

Now, all of this mess
Will get into the air,
Just think of the sky,
And please say you care.

So, send me some help.
I'm falling behind,
And please use your doohickeys
More than one time.

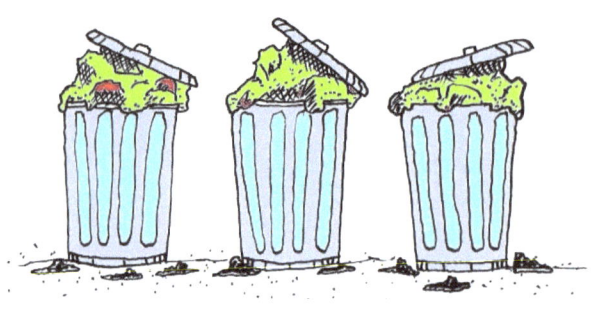

Garbage

I hate taking out the garbage.
   They should make a law.
You should have to wear special gloves,
   And a plastic suit and all.

I wouldn't have to take out the garbage,
   Each and every day;
It would save me so much grief,
   If you didn't throw so much away.

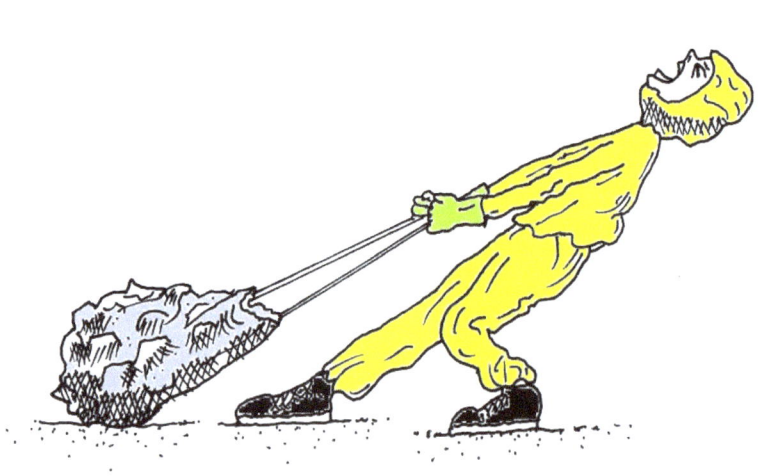

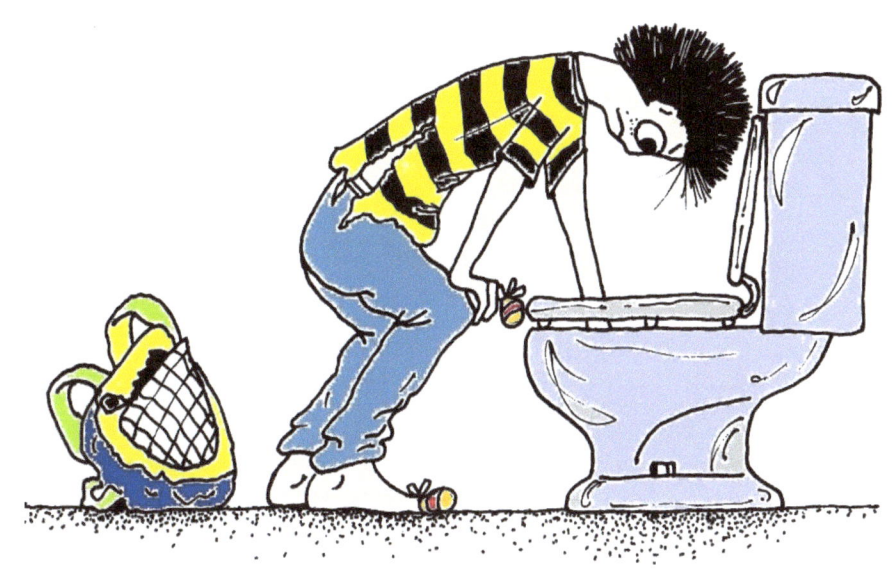

A New Day

I stubbed my toe on the bed,
And smashed my finger in the drawer.
I tore my shirt on the chair,
And spilled my milk on the floor.

My toothbrush fell in the toilet,
And I can't get my backpack open.
Can I please have a new day?
This one seems to be broken.

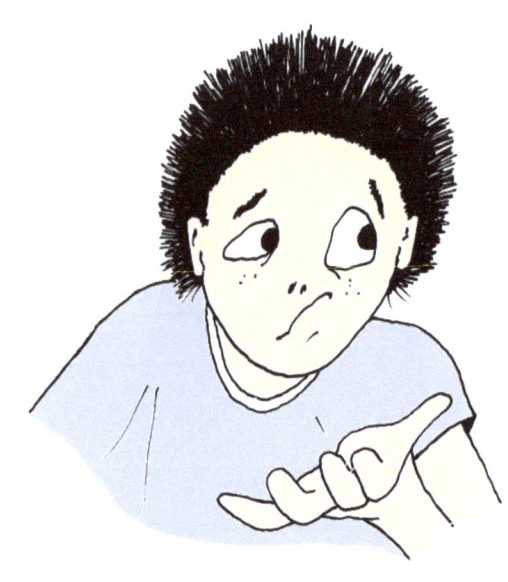

Being Good Is Hard

I'm trying to do what's right;
Be nice to my brother and sister,
Pick up all my toys,
And try not to bother or pester,

Be polite to people,
And do things in a proper way.
But being good is hard.
I know, I tried it yesterday.

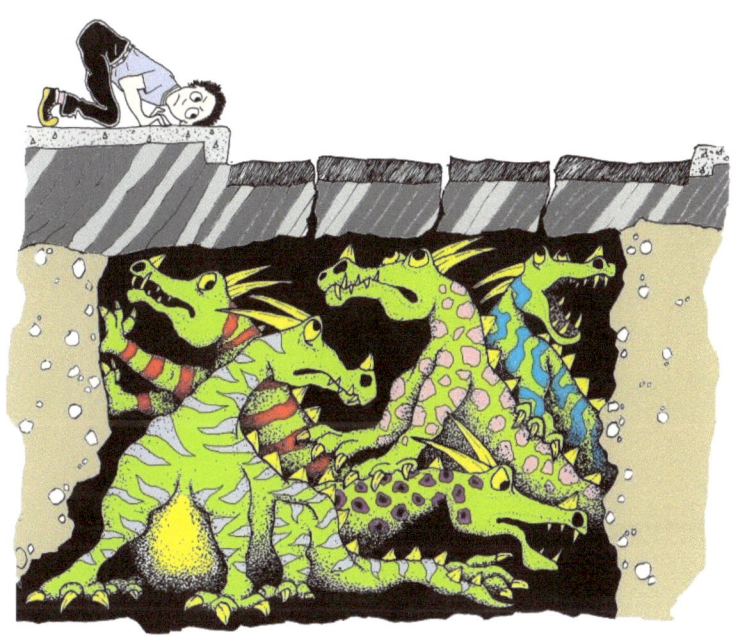

Dragons Underneath

There are cracks in the asphalt
That weren't there before.
People better be careful,
Or someone could get sore.

Now, if you listen real closely,
And put your ear to the ground,
You can hear something moving,
Like things bumping around.

Now my Dad says the cracks
Are from the sun's terrible heat.
But, I know why the asphalt's cracked;
There are dragons

        underneath.

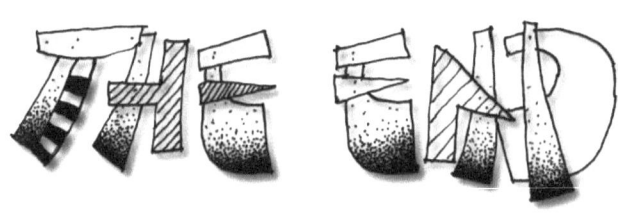

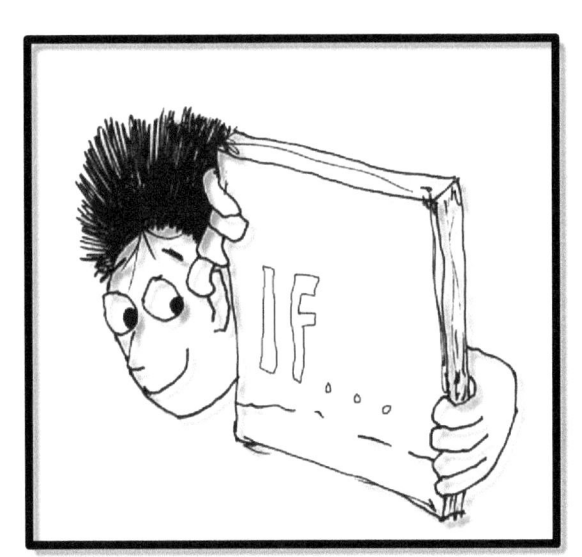

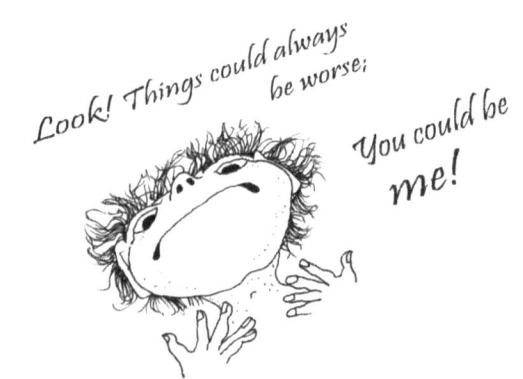

www.ingramcontent.com/pod-product-compliance
Lightning Source LLC
Chambersburg PA
CBHW051211220526
45473CB00003B/993